WONDER WIDOWS

TRISH COMER • PEGGY LANGENWALTER • JENNIFER COX-HORAK

PRAISE FOR
WONDER WIDOWS

"This book is a much needed treat for the widow's lonely soul. The stories of Trish, Peggy, and Jennifer's strength and resilience, and their ability to heal and start anew in the face of the ups and downs and pains and heartaches that come with the loss of a spouse are *revivifying*. It's liberating to finally understand that this loss is not the destination, it's not the end of the story, it's a part of a journey that could be the mere seeds of an *amazing* beginning."
—**Homayoun Sadeghi, MD., ob/gyn physician and author of**
The Art of Healthy Living

"*Wonder Widows* captures the pain to power journey of three women who came together after the loss of their husbands. Their processes throughout their journeys through these heartbreaking losses and their grief are skillfully organized and listed to help the reader navigate the grieving process. I wish this book had been available to guide me in the loss of my husband and in counseling my clients through the world of pain, loss and transformation after the death of a spouse. Now, *Wonder Widows* and the hope of promise of change are here to facilitate the journey for the reader."
—**Joan Dalton-Boyd, M.A., Grief and Transition Counselor and**
educator

"Grief can cause such an imbalance not only in the physical body, but for the mind, emotions and spirit. It's good to read about the many different ways the authors developed their own unique self-care plan. There truly isn't a one-size-fits-all plan!"
—**Christiane Northrup, M.D.**, ob/gyn physician and author of
the *New York Times* bestsellers *Goddesses Never Age, Women's Bodies, Women's Wisdom,* and *The Wisdom of Menopause*

"It is so inspiring to read how these three courageous widows have not allowed grief to stop them from moving forward in life. I hope their heartfelt stories and life lessons provide solace and comfort to women and men who like me, journeyed to find understanding, wisdom, and strength. Know that there are many of us who share in this struggle and our bond, cemented in the love for those we've lost will see us through."

—Governor Michelle Lujan Grisham, New Mexico

"*Wonder Widows* is written with depth, honesty and sensitivity. The unique stories that Trish, Peggy and Jennifer share are truly inspirational for all widows who wish to rediscover the joy in living."

—Weam Namou, award-winning author of 13 books, including *Healing Wisdom for a Wounded World* and *Mesopotamian Goddesses: Unveiling Your Feminine Power*

"Authors Trish Comer, Peggy Langenwalter & Jennifer Cox-Horak are not only friends and neighbors, all three are widows, each with their own unique story to share. Together, and with significant sacrifice, Trish, Peggy, and Jennifer will escort you, the reader, through the grief gauntlet they traveled and the countless best practices they learned during the days following their loss. From having intuitions about their husband's death to his funeral arrangements to relations with family and friends to their emotional pain and personal challenges, these three Wonder Widows hold nothing back. Candid, direct and on-point, each page of *Wonder Widows* encourages the reader to read on. Be sure to have a yellow highlighter handy. Whether a woman is a caregiver for her terminally ill spouse or a recent widow (or not so new widow), you'll want to read the *Wonder Widows.*"

—Herb Knoll, author *of The Widowers Journey* **and Founder of Widowers Support Network**

Life is short, live it.
Love is rare, grab it.
Anger is bad, dump it.
Fear is awful, face it.
Memories are sweet,
Cherish them.

-Unknown

CONTENTS

DEDICATION

We dedicate this labor of love in book form to many important people.

Foremost, we recognize the contributions our spouses made to our lives and our journey as widows. With enduring love, we acknowledge our husbands: Bob (Trish), Dan (Peggy), and Chuck (Jennifer).

We also recognize the meaningful role our children have played in our journey through grief and into a new life of hope and joy. We love you and thank you sincerely.

Our grandchildren have helped us focus on the present and the future. They lend purpose, relevance, and meaning to our lives. Our precious young ones also occupy hours of our time that might otherwise feel empty. Hugs and kisses to you.

The understanding and attention of our siblings has been invaluable. We salute you for your steadfast support.

Friends who stood by us in ways large and small played an important role in helping us find our footing in a strange, new world. In your honor, we will pass your kindness onto others in their time of need.

To authors of the books we devoured who shared words of wisdom and healing, we say thank you.

To anyone not specifically mentioned who made up a vital part of our band of helpers, we extend our heartfelt gratitude.

Thoughts of you
Don't fill my head
With music
As once before.

Just whispers of remorse
For that which was once
Can not be once more.

Yet, in the chambers of my mind
Your steps echo hauntingly
And I'll visit the glow
You left behind
If only occasionally.

I simply stand
And watch your smile
Fading now with time
And wonder at the dimness,
Perhaps not too unkind.

-Connie Edwards, Albuquerque, NM

ACKNOWLEDGEMENTS

We wish to say thank you to Trish's daughter, Räna Doyal, for her artistic hand. With the book cover she designed, she captured our hopes that we can break the silence of widowhood and help other widows feel as empowered as we've learned to feel.

Peggy and I would like to thank our co-writer and artist, Jennifer, for the adorable sketches of our heads, and Räna Doyal for putting them on powerful bodies.

We very much want to recognize that contributing to this body of work was intensely difficult for our grown children as well. Each child put off writing for quite a few months, not wanting to pull the scab off the wound, so to speak. Eventually, out of respect for Mom and Dad, they did complete the assignment and we are exceedingly grateful.

We send a very special thank you to Gloriann for sharing her tips with us. Gloriann married Peggy's father three years after Peggy's mother passed away. She is a gentle, wise, and loving soul who excels in compassion and holds several degrees in counseling. She herself has outlived three husbands. When Gloriann arrived from out of town for Dan's funeral celebration, she brought some very helpful information to share with Peggy and her family and friends. We've included that information in this book for your personal use. Gloriann gathered the information from several hospices and grief groups.

You will find Gloriann's tips in Appendix III & IV.

We wish to acknowledge our editor, Tiffany Cole, for her patience, sensitivity, and dedication to helping us edit this book. Her support contributed to keeping us on a timeline so this project could reach completion. We sincerely appreciate Tiffany's professional expertise.

We wish to thank Stacey Blake, our book formatter, for her tremendous amount of patience with us throughout the layout and design process.

VISITORS OF ALIVENESS

—Matt Licata, PhD
www.mattlicataphd.com
reprinted with permission

There are times when the ground has fallen away, and there are no longer any reference points from which to make sense of what is happening. The narratives are conflicting, the feelings are contradictory, and the path forward is hazy. It's as if you can't access what was so clear from even a few days ago. All of the work you've done—surrendering, the healing, the forgiving, the realizations, the staying in the now...for some reason, it's no longer in reach. It's as if you're being asked to start over.

While the mind will interpret the starting over as failure, inside the heart it is sacred. Love is always asking you to start over, in each moment to return into the naked, tender, erupting purity of the unknown.

There is a sense that some sort of veil is parting, but what is coming next has not yet been given. At times the unknown feels like such a creative place, but at other times it is disorienting there, and the yearning for resolution burns through your body. A certain death has come, and you know that things will never be the same. But the rebirth has not yet appeared, and the longing for ground is rippling through you.

Rather than struggle against the uncertainty, the invitation is to rest inside it. There is a sanctuary there, though it is hidden and may not be accessible via ordinary means. But you can reach it through a portal inside your heart. Look there. While the mind may spin during times of bardo and reorganization, the body knows…the heart knows. Go there.

Stay close to what is alive now, even if what is there is flat, numb and confused. For these are special visitors of aliveness, and operate outside conventional awareness. They serve to open and close dimensions of your vulnerability that have fallen outside your reach.

Listen carefully to the invitation, as it arrives in thundering silence. Today may not be a day for answers, but to let your heart break open to the vastness of the question.

REFLECTIONS

I looked into the full-length mirror mounted on the bathroom wall of my childhood home filled with memories. To enter and exit the bathtub and shower, one must step in front of the mirror totally nude, perfectly honest, and facing the truth.

The eyes looking back at me were not the wide, innocent eyes of the thirteen year old who wondered when her skinny, boyish body would respond to the changing ratio of hormones she'd been told about.

They were not the admiring and curious eyes of that fifteen year old who paused for just a moment, appreciating the soft curves that Mother Nature was beginning to bestow on her.

The brown eyes in the mirror were not the eyes of the seventeen year old who gratefully accepted the full breasts and broad hips that were now completely hers. That young woman, having caught sight of her undisguised reflection, felt passion ignite and dared to wonder what pleasures this new form might bring her and her beloved someday.

They were not the eyes of the young mother taking note of her breasts, heavy with life-sustaining fluid, and a tummy slightly rounder and softer than before. These eyes acknowledged, with thankfulness, a body that had performed brilliantly when called upon to perpetuate the species.

They were not the eyes of the grieving, seasoned woman who stepped into the shower to let the soothing water dilute her sorrow and rejuvenate her spirit.

Rather, they were the steady eyes of a woman who had begun to tread confidently on the footpath of her sage years. Life's joys and disappointments had left their mark on her heart and caused her eyes to shine with wisdom. Where there had been judgment, there was now acceptance. Where there had been fear, there was faith. Where there had been greed, there was gratitude. Where there had been pride in ownership, there was peace in sharing.

These were the eyes, indeed, of a matron who had engaged in the dance of birthing a baby and birthing a soul. They had witnessed life beginning and life ending. They had observed the first breath and the last breath.

They were the eyes of a woman who could unwaveringly and unapologetically stand in front of the ever-truthful mirror and drink in the sight of her loyal body, complete with modifications her genuine life had left as mementos. The distortions and scars she views are evidence that she is fully living life, accepting the consequences of the choices she makes.

These are the eyes of a woman who anticipates the inevitable senior years while steadfastly retaining a graceful grip on a shadow of her youth.

The eyes looking back at me have shed tears of delight and tears of sadness. They have seen the comedy and the tragedy of life.

They are windows into a life boldly lived. They are smiling contentedly and they are mine.

Peggy McClarin Langenwalter
February 4, 2006
Written while staying at my childhood home
One week after Dad's memorial service in La Luz, NM

LOVE YOU DIFFERENT

When Herb Knoll was about sixty years old and while he was out for one of his evening walks, he began considering what the future may hold in store for him as a widower. While he didn't believe he could ever love another woman after Michelle's passing, over time, he came to understand how the human heart is capable of loving more than once. It then occurred to him how given his age, any chance of falling in love again may very well be with a widow.

Herb decided to pen some lyrics, after which he set them aside for several years. Then one day, he approached three of his dear and gifted friends—Kim Parent, Rob Harris, and Marcia Ramirez—each a Nashville based singer-songwriter, to see if they would be interested in helping him bring "Love You Different" to life. Thankfully so, they did. "Love You Different" is available on iTunes.

The first time Herb shared the song with Peggy, Jennifer, and me, it brought tears to our eyes—not tears of sadness, but tears of hope that one day we will share a different love with someone that understands and accepts our loss. We wish to share that hope with you.

Yes, one day our hearts can love again—a different love.

"Love You Different"

I have come to know
The heart can love again
Even after true love has passed into the wind
There's no need to explain
What you're going through
'Cause not long ago, I lost an angel, too
I know you miss him
But I'll love you different
I won't replace him or want you to forget
You'll never love the same
That's not for me to change
I know you miss him
But I'll love you different

Even as we let them go
Part of them will stay
Woven deep into our lives and who we are today
That's something we can celebrate
So let me wipe your tears away, my beautiful friend
I believe they'd tell us it's okay to love again

-Lyrics by Knoll, Harris, Ramirez & Parent

INTRODUCTION

When you were in a relationship, once in a while you may have wondered who would go first and then dismissed the thought as quickly as it had appeared. Sometimes you caught yourself glancing at an older widow and thinking, "At least they had a lot of years together."

And then it happened to *you*!

Everyday life as you knew it ended after his last breath. The familiar world you knew just moments before ceased to exist, and a new door opened into a vast unknown world.

Your heart ached. Your tears flowed uncontrollably. You turned back, looking for the door that once contained your life, the life that was brimming with accumulated experiences and memories between you and your loved one.

Then one day you put one foot in front of the other and began the search for new bearings. Day by day, you started noticing the dark clouds parting and a ray of sunshine and hope peeking through.

Life isn't over. A new beginning has just revealed itself. Death can be a wakeup call to life. It's an opportunity to rediscover the joy of living while incorporating the experience of grief into the fabric of your newly created life.

You, dear reader, are not alone on your journey. We are with you.

Who are we? Allow me, Trish, to introduce the Wonder Widows.

We are three widows that came together quite naturally. We didn't meet at a grief support meeting. It just so happens Peggy is a neighbor of my daughter Räna, who introduced us when Peggy had been a widow for about eighteen months and I was still married to my husband, Bob. We realized we had many common interests. We both practice and teach well-being and healthy living. It only seemed natural to invite Jennifer, a friend of mine, into our developing writing group, as she also shares our interests.

As we move through this process, just like you, we step closer to a place of peace that radiates within and without. We've learned to love ourselves and others. We've learned to forgive ourselves and others. From the dark depths of grief, we move toward the shining heights of resilience. As we travel from sorrow to acceptance, we move toward peace and liberation.

While we recognized the depth of true human emotions, we also recognized we didn't want to get stuck in the sadness and drag it into our future lives. We knew processing grief and mourning wasn't the destination; it was simply a necessary part of the journey of our lives.

From tragedy and loss, we have learned to thrive, and we want to help you thrive as well.

Peggy fell for her prince charming, Dan, while working a summer job where her father was employed and married him at eighteen. Due to a tragic accident, she lost her husband of forty-two years in an instant when he fell from a high ladder while putting some finishing touches on the new home they'd designed in preparation of their retirement and their happy golden years together. Peggy has been learning to thrive in her own unique way since 2012.

Jennifer met her soul mate, Chuck, through mutual friends as destiny would have it. She fell in love and they eloped on April Fool's Day in 2004. Our dear Jennifer, a young woman pregnant with their second child, watched her husband succumb to the wrath of pancreatic cancer over a period of a few short months. Jennifer was a new widow when she gave birth to Charlie Ann, named in honor of the father the baby would not know. Jennifer has been learning to thrive in her own unique way since 2010. Jennifer found herself very involved in the care of her two young children, who did not have a father. Due to serious family responsibilities, she chose to become a contributing writer, and we thank her for being a part of this book.

And then there is me, Trish…

I recognized that Bob was my soul mate at first glance. He was fulfilling a college internship requirement for his degree at the same location where I was facilitating training for volunteers at a local youth service bureau. We fell in love and became engaged just one month later and married five months after that. My husband of thirty-six years and I were preparing for our second half of life. We were just making inroads with our nonprofit organization and trying to find the time to finish up several manuscripts when he passed away over a three-month period that consisted of multiple doctors failing to diagnose a painful and debilitating illness. I can say with certainty that my husband and I had both started new journeys, albeit very different and apart from one another. I have been learning to thrive in my own unique way since 2014.

The three of us gathered around a dining room table in the comfort and security of Peggy's home while sharing our most intimate thoughts and feelings. Our friendship deepened each time we met to share our experiences. We cried and laughed and bonded. After all, who better understands the journey than other widows?

However, there was a surprise awaiting us that we didn't see coming. We didn't realize how challenging individually typing the draft of our stories would be. Our hearts were being tugged and pulled as we relived the memories. We found ourselves alone with our thoughts and memories and without the comfort and support of our widow friends.

At times we would have to put the word processor away for long stretches and rest. We would pick up the writing at a later date once we felt we were strong enough to continue. However, we began to see there was a silver lining in this difficult writing task. We began to notice we were not looking back with such heavy emotions. Instead, we found the more we shared in our writing, the more we were healing. The writing helped put things in better perspective. We made a few phone calls to each other, renewed our determination to finish the book, took deep breaths, and moved forward.

Why did we write this book?

We are not grief counselors, nor are we psychologists. We are three women who came together with a common purpose. We want to share how we are learning to thrive in this new world as we process our grief. You will surely see parts of your own story in the stories we share about our challenges, our triumphs, and our anticipations of the future. We want to encourage you to thrive. We are here to inspire you and perhaps to help empower you to break the silence and isolation of widowhood. We view widowhood as a journey, not a destination. Through this book, we want to offer you inspiration, comfort, compassion, camaraderie, and friendship. We invite you to travel with us as we rediscover the joy of living while also incorporating the experience of grief into the fabric of our new lives.

As we move through this process, we step closer to a place of peace within that radiates without. We write this book as part of our own process. If our experiences benefit others, that's a bonus.

This book is also written for friends and family who care deeply for a grieving widow and wish to have greater insight into her journey.

We will frankly answer questions such as whether we still wear our wedding ring and what we think about sex now that we are single women. We also discuss our deepest thoughts and the guiding philosophies that are helping us move forward.

We are the Wonder Widows—thriving, strong, and resilient as we create a new normal.

Come, sit at the table with us!

TRISH

PEGGY

JENNIFER

CHAPTER ONE

Did You Feel It Coming?
Interesting intuitions, premonitions or conversations
before death or illness

TRISH

During the evening of July 30, 2014, while visiting Bob during
his first of two hospital visits, I watched looming dark clouds
move in from the North over Albuquerque from his hospital room. Shortly thereafter, a violent thunderstorm erupted.
Once it passed, I kissed my husband goodbye and headed
home only to catch a glimpse of the start of a magnificent
sunset. Brilliantly bright sunbeams appeared as though they
could touch the ground and pierced through the remaining
puffy dark clouds. It was a scene from a biblical picture. It was
in that moment my intuition handed me a strong dose of bad
news that my husband of thirty-six years could really be preparing to die. Tears welled up in my eyes, making it difficult
to navigate the familiar road that I had been accustomed to
driving for many days.

Just a couple of weeks before, a lighter dose of intuition

struck me while I prepared for a visit from my sister and dad from Chicago on July 15, 2014. Even though Bob's health seemed to be deteriorating, we still didn't have a diagnosis and we were waiting for the results of a MRI. While he lay on the couch, I was hit with some pretty big household maintenance to take care of. When I raised the blinds in the seldom used guest room, I discovered a rain-damaged wall just below the window. I had to replaster it, and of course, I had to restucco the damaged wall outside—the origin of the problem. I re-called thinking, "I feel like a widow!" The feeling was fairly strong, but out of necessity I had to dismiss it because of my lengthy to-do list.

While driving to greet my relatives at the downtown train station, Bob received good news. His doctor felt fairly certain Bob had autoimmune pancreatitis and a dose of ste-roids would return him to health. That evening while at a lo-cal restaurant, we felt we had more to celebrate than just the arrival of our guests. We were also celebrating a diagnosis and what appeared to be a treatable illness, or so we thought. While walking out of the restaurant bathroom with my sister, I said to her, "I'm feeling so relieved to have Bob's diagnosis. I thought for a while I was going to be a widow soon."

About one month before Bob became ill, we were talking about the ashes of a friend's recently deceased mother. I ca-sually asked if he'd thought about where he wanted his ashes spread if he died before me. Without any hesitation, he said he had thought about it and described the location as being the most peaceful and beautiful place he'd ever been. I would have bet a million dollars that he was going to say Hawaii, where we had spent seventeen days in paradise when renewing our vows for our twenty-fifth wedding anniversary! I was shocked when he said that he wanted his ashes spread off the coast of the Makah Indian reservation. Makah is located on the tip of the state of Washington where the Puget Sound meets the Pacific Ocean. He asked me where I would want my ashes spread, and I said I hadn't thought about it. It never crossed my mind. His quick response haunted me all day, as I had a strange feeling he was going to go before me. I did my best to try and dismiss it.

For years while Bob was alive, I had extraordinarily vivid dreams in the future tense. However, I began noticing a pattern about the dreams. They did not include Bob (with the exception of only one rare dream), and it disturbed me very much. I had to be so careful with my wording when sharing the dreams of the future with him. I really wanted him to be there with me, but nevertheless, the feeling he would not be in my future would haunt me for the better part of each following day.

PEGGY

There were a few interesting occurrences preceding Dan's death. The first one was about a month after my friend had died by suicide. I remember sitting up in bed one morning. Dan was out of bed, getting ready for work. I'd said, "He was such a good man. He was a good man. He was polite and kind and thoughtful." Dan could see how sad I was and he came over, very tenderly touched my face, and said, "I'm not going anywhere." At the time I thought, "That is really sweet, you are my rock and I need you, but why would you even say that? Of course you're not going anywhere." He could have just been trying to reassure me, but that struck me as being a little odd. I didn't expect him to say that because I knew he wasn't going anywhere. This happened about eight months before Dan died.

On a Saturday morning, about two weeks before I left on a business trip, he had gotten up just a little before me. He had showered and gotten dressed, and he was standing in the hallway near our open bedroom door. As I sat up in bed, a strange feeling came over me. I said, "Dan…"

"Yes?"

"Your mother died at sixty-five."

"Yes."

"Your dad died at sixty-five."

"Mmm hmm."

"You're sixty-five."

He was silent for a few seconds, drew in a deep breath, and said with happy enthusiasm, "Yeah, and I'm *so* much healthier than they were!"

He knew he was healthy, he knew he was strong, and he knew everything was fine. We both did. He'd just had a thorough check-up with his doctor a few days before and had received a clean bill of health.

A year or two before, Dan had stated, "Well, my mom died at sixty-five, my dad died at sixty-five, I'm getting close to sixty-five…"

I'd jumped into his thoughts. "Don't you even think that way! We are—*you* are—healthy, you are strong, and we don't live like your parents. Their lifestyle was so different from ours. Don't even get that thought in your head."

That was that. When the words came out of my mouth a couple years later, I thought, "Why did that come out of my mouth?" That's not the way I think.

The next day, we were in the kitchen. It was Sunday morning. Dan was sitting at the island, and I was walking around behind him as I cleared breakfast dishes.

He suddenly asked, "Are you happy?"

It was not our habit to ask each other that question, so that struck me as funny. I said, "Yes."

He asked, "How happy are you?"

I said, "Very happy."

He asked, "What do you tell people?"

"What do you mean?" I asked.

"What do you tell your girlfriends about me?"

That was interesting. I said, "I tell people you are a wonderful man and that you're a wonderful husband and that you take very good care of me."

He responded, "Oh." He seemed content.

I stopped clearing dishes for a moment and asked, "What about you, Dan? Are you happy?"

He said yes, and I asked, "How happy?"

With great enthusiasm, he answered, "I'm *very* happy."

Within a few days, he was gone, and it comforted me that we'd had that conversation. He knew I was happy and very much in love with him, and I knew he was happy and very much in love with me. Remembering that conversation has given me peace.

Anniversary roses arrived one week before our forty-second anniversary, two weeks before he died, with a sweet note. "It seems we've been celebrating this anniversary for months. I've enjoyed every minute. I love you."

Dan left Monday morning to work out of town, and he would be coming home on Friday. Before he left, we hugged and kissed and said good-bye. As he was leaving, I told him, "I'll see you Sunday. I look forward to being back here with you."

On Thursday of that same week, I also had to leave town for business. My bags were packed, and I was getting ready to leave. I wanted the house to look absolutely pristine when Dan walked in Friday afternoon. We loved our new home. It was a labor of love that we had created together, along with our wonderful builder. We were still in the process of moving out of our previous house. We still had boxes to unpack, but the house was beginning to feel like home. I wanted to clean every piece of lint, every little water drop. I'm sure it was my way of honoring Dan and his sacrifices to get us into this beautiful, new home.

I polished up the kitchen and went into the powder room. After I polished up the faucet and the sink in the powder room, I started to walk out to tidy another room. As I approached the door, it felt as though an unseen force had stopped me. I stopped in my tracks. Again, it was as though unseen hands had tilted my head until I was looking at the skylight. I heard myself say out loud, "Dan's going to try to clean that before I get home."

The weekend before, Dan had cleaned paint off the skylight in our master bathroom. He had taken a ladder in there and had done it while I was making breakfast. When he came out, I asked, "Did you go up on that ladder? You didn't call me."

He said, "Uh, it just takes me a few seconds. I just climb up and scrape it off and I'm down again, no sweat."

I continued making my point. "You know, even though we feel strong, we need to have spotters now. In fact, we need to have people come over and do that. I will call the superintendent to come and clean the paint off of the skylights, so don't do that anymore."

And he said, "Oh, Peggy, they are so busy and they need

to be building new houses because that is how they make their money. You know I can take care of this."

Coming back to the present moment as I was preparing to leave for the airport, I thought about Dan's determination to clean the paint off the skylights. I knew he was doing it out of love for me. He wanted the house to be complete and finished for me. Our love and respect for each other, our desire to honor the other, was mutual.

I didn't get a feeling that I needed to call him and warn him again to stay off the ladder. I went to my closet, got my suitcase, and was rolling it around the corner in the hall. Once again, I was stopped in my tracks. I became aware of a gossamer thought passing through my mind about being a widow, like someone was having a conversation with me. I realized it when the words that came out of my mouth were, "What *would* happen if Dan died?" I answered myself aloud. "I'd be a widow." I paused, took a breath, and said, "I'm glad I don't have to think about that for another twenty years."

That Thursday I continued on my way, loaded my suitcase into the trunk of the car, and drove to the airport. The next day, Dan returned home. Saturday afternoon, he climbed up on a ladder to clean the paint off the skylight in the powder room, fell, and was gone in an instant. I was out of town and he was alone. No goodbyes. Just the phone call no one wants to get.

JENNIFER

Seems to me that yes, I did have a premonition of sorts about things to come. The first real fight Chuck and I ever got into was pretty intense. Of course, me being the highly sensitive, emotional creature that I am, I can easily recall that moment of complete hurt I'd felt after such a serious, male-dominated argument. I sat on the front porch of our little bungalow in Austin, Texas, crying, realizing after a little over a year with this man that I'd never truly be rid of him unless he died. Chuck was such a strong-minded man, which played a strong role in his unwillingness to change his lifestyle or patterns for anyone other than himself. The thing is, I was so enamored with him that I knew in my heart I wouldn't leave willingly. I was completely under his persuasion, as he was mine, or at least that's what I'd like to believe based on our experiences together.

We came to Albuquerque for a few reasons. One being, I wanted to study Ayurveda, and I did so with Dr. Lad. Ayurveda is very fascinating because it involves using the whole mind, body, spirit connection to maintain and improve the health of the human body. Chuck had a back ache that never seemed to get better. After finishing a year at the Ayurvedic Institute, I had come to understand that when the body has persistent aches, it's a sign of imbalance or disease. For close to two years, I asked Chuck to have it checked out. As most men say: "Oh, it's nothing but age and work-related stress."

I kept asking, and I even tried to trick him into seeing a doctor about this constant pain in his lower part of his back. I knew something wasn't right, and I might have even thought about that dreaded feeling I had the night of our first real fight. I chose not to think any more about the possibility of death because, you know, death only happens to those who suddenly get in an accident or the elderly. Yeah, I know there is no truth to that; it was just that I couldn't imagine Chuck dying, especially from cancer. Hell, I thought the man would get beat to death over some wacked out road rage incident.

The premonition didn't sink in until it was revealed to me on a spiritual level the night before Chuck died. Deep down I had heard all the whispers from the medical professionals as they came in and out of the hospital room, but I kept holding on to the faith that he and I could be that miracle story you hear about from someone's mother, brother-in-law, or cousin's friend where the ill beats some horrific terminal illness. Chuck suffered as all cancer victims seem to. I was afraid to touch him sometimes in fear that it might be too painful for him.

The day before he passed, I remember sitting with him on the hospice bed in the early morning while holding his hand and sending him my love, just being present with him, when it hit me how hard he was fighting to stay alive for me, Hayden, and little Miss Charlie Anne. I held his hand while sobbing and I told him we'd find our way and that it was time for him to leave.

I couldn't allow him to suffer anymore because of my selfish attachment to him. I don't know how long I sat on the bed with him. I wanted him to feel Charlie Anne kicking around in my belly just like all expectant fathers should be doing before their baby's arrival. It all seems so silly how my thinking was then. I have no idea how much awareness he had for the physical world around him, but I just kept on believing he knew what needed to be known.

That evening, he had rolled around in the bed and I was exhausted. Nora—Chuck's mom—and I had been taking turns watching after Chuck during the nights so that we could have some kind of rest. I never really did—or have again, for that matter—sleep peacefully. This particular night was going to be my turn, so I decided that I would rest on the bed as long as I could before I became the night nurse. Somewhere between deep sleep and awake, I felt Chuck walk into the room. I'm lying there knowing I'm asleep just enough that this couldn't be real, but it felt so real. I never moved, but my perspective did as if my head was turning to follow him. There he stood next to the bed, and he looked so vibrant, healthy, and beautiful.

He said to me, "Baby, it's so good." I could feel the tears start streaming down my sleeping face and I said, "No. It's because you're there and I'm still here." I jolted up to grab him one last time, but he was gone. It felt like it was just a dream. I'd like to believe that it was one of those momentary glimpses of all that is beyond this physical world. I'm certain that this experience will be argued as fantasy. I, however, believe in the magic of the world and I know it was him trying to tell me not to be afraid for him. I know this as my truth. It was, and still is, so very real.

CHAPTER TWO

Cremation or Burial?
Dealing with the decision of what to do with the body

TRISH

We always knew we wanted our bodies to be cremated for environmental reasons and per our spiritual philosophy that our bodies just carry us in the physical world, but our soul will always live on. Therefore, I carried out his wishes by cremating him.

PEGGY

Because we had recently been caretakers for Dan's ninety-three-year-old aunt, Jenny, and we had made many end-of-life decisions with her, this was a topic we were familiar with. Plus, we had experience with friends and family who had died in the past. We did not hesitate to talk about death or how to handle the remains. We agreed about the wisdom of organ donation, body donation, and cremation.

The day we donated Dan's organs was a very bad day for

our family, but a very happy and fortunate day for people we would never meet. That's the gift of life and health. That's how it goes.

My good friends Elena and John were in town to support me. John accompanied me to the crematorium. Ten months before, I had visited this same crematorium to make arrangements for Aunt Jenny's cremation. Never did I guess I would be there again ten short months later. Actually, I was devastated to be there again. I felt like a robot with eyes that could not stop pouring tears. I very much needed John's help and emotional strength to get through this ordeal.

To this day, I have Dan's ashes in a box in a closet. In the few weeks after Dan's death, I asked our sons if they wanted some of Dan's ashes. Each son declined. Perhaps someday my three sons and I, and maybe other close friends and relatives, will take a hike to one of Dan's favorite places and ceremoniously deposit his ashes in a spot that holds special meaning.

JENNIFER

Thank goodness Chuck had always talked about cremation and his desire to be cremated because honestly, grieving so intensely while pregnant will leave a woman more than half-crazed. Humorously, I very well could have stuffed him and set him up on the sofa like he was listening to music just to have what was left of what I knew of him there. I could then continue nursing some insane delusion that he had never really died and that this all had never really happened. It was the love of friends and family that kept me from a mental institution. I'm six and a half years into grieving, and there are still triggers that set off intense grieving. It sucks!

Well, to give you all peace of mind, I didn't stuff him. I let go of all control and released it to the universe while accepting unconditionally the help that was offered, as I felt it was needed. This is where Nora, Chuck's mom, stepped up. I wonder if she ever realized there was no way I could've afforded to have him buried in his family plot in East Texas. I didn't even really care where or if he was going to be buried because in my heart I knew all that I loved was gone and what I had left was an old vehicle ready for impound. So, Nora took care of the cremation. I went and picked up the shoe box of what was left of my lover, my closest friend and the father of my children. It's crazy to think of a six-foot-two, two-hundred-pound man in a box the size tennis shoes come in.

CHAPTER THREE

---www---

Memorial or Celebration of Life?
Somber or celebratory

TRISH

The kids and I planned a Celebration of Life close to what would have been his sixty-first birthday in September partly due to not wanting to face "the first" birthday without him. We had a grand turnout of about seventy-some people. I created a large playlist of Bob's favorite classic rock music, which was played throughout the event. Dinner consisted of his favorite BBQ food and some of his other favorite foods. I must have made twenty pounds of potato salad, and our daughter Räna made a pot of her famous green chile stew. Of course we had his favorite imported beer to wash it all down! We provided magic markers and helium balloons for the family and guests so they could write a wish for Bob on the balloons and release them to the night sky later in the evening. For me that was a somber and yet a very heartwarming tribute to my husband, the father of our two children.

Most of our extended family lives in the Chicago area, so

we planned a second Celebration of Life in May in the Chicago area to coincide with what would have been our thirty-seventh wedding anniversary, another one of those "first" milestones that I wasn't prepared to face. Four and a half months after Bob's passing, my "other rock," my father, passed away peacefully on January 7, 2015. We happily combined the two celebrations. We had my father's in the morning with a military theme that included a gun salute performed by his brother, Tom. In the afternoon, we had more of a rock 'n' roll theme that my good friend, musician Sarah Allen organized for us with a band. Besides immediate and extended family, quite a few of Bob's friends attended that I hadn't seen in a very long time as well as my friends from college. That reunion really showed me, and I'm sure our friends, just how precious life is and that it should not be taken for granted.

PEGGY

We had a Celebration of Life. Although it was a sad occasion, there was happiness and laughter, too.

Even with the fog that had settled over our hearts and brains, the celebration six days after Dan's fall came together nicely. Our daughter-in-law took charge and wrote the obituary and got it announced in the paper. Some friends we hadn't seen for thirty years came to the celebration because they saw the announcement. That was sweet.

We held the standing-room-only service in a country club event room. It was a touching event attended by friends and colleagues of ours who came from far and near. I was aware that these kind people came with only a few days' notice, some driving, some flying, and all having changed their busy schedules to attend and honor Dan and lend us support.

Our son, Kyle, organized the event and did a great job emceeing. Each of our sons spoke, offering loving words about their father and gratitude to those in attendance. Several close friends spoke. I was the last speaker. I talked about how fully Dan lived life while traveling and going on countless adventures by Jeep as the driver, sailboat as the captain, and private plane as the pilot. I explained that at his time of death, Dan was loving life and the people in it. He also knew he was very much loved and appreciated in return. I thanked everyone for coming on short notice to share their love for Dan and for our family. I respectfully asked people to refrain from telling us "Dan's in a better place" or "It was his time to go" or other words meant to comfort us that our hearts could not draw comfort from just yet. I explained that I was exhausted, and I hoped they would understand if I slipped out the door after the service.

Our son, Noah, is involved in barbershop singing and at one point toward the end of the celebration, his barbershop friends, who were scattered throughout the crowd, broke out in song to the surprise and delight of the other guests. In beautiful and stirring four-part harmony, men sang the Irish Blessing. It was beautiful, and it was a wonderful touch to the happy celebration.

Irish Blessing

May the road rise to meet you,
May the wind be always at your back.
May the sun shine warm upon your face,
The rains fall soft upon your fields.
And until we meet again,
May God hold you in the palm of his hand.

As the song came to an end, my three sons surrounded me protectively and guided me and my sister out of the building and into Dan's truck. Birk, our youngest son who was looking smart in his Navy uniform that would surely make his dad proud, slid into the driver's seat and drove Rita and me home. Our energy was spent as we quietly waited for others to arrive for a family dinner and pay tribute to the man we were missing.

JENNIFER

I didn't do jack crap! Did I or do I feel guilty? No. I'm telling you, I didn't have the capacity to function beyond putting one foot in front of the other. My life had become nothing but intense fear. I was completely focused on survival and my desperate need to sleep in preparation for Charlie Anne's birth, so if someone wasn't willing to do some type of ceremony, I knew one wouldn't happen. Those things cost money, and well, I didn't have any which left the financing and planning up to Chuck's family. After hearing one or two complaints from some of Chuck's more distant friends, I decided to have a coming out party for Charlie Anne sometime after she was born. It included honoring her father. It was a nice turnout, and the party helped to emphasize the positive aspects of his legacy.

I don't know why, but life can feel pretty crazy most of the time for us younger widows. However, we make it through the ups and downs in all the ways we choose to respond to each circumstance. What keeps me grounded is that I know who really loves me and our children, and that's the important part. The more I read through these questions and think about my responses to certain situations, the more I realize the important role hormones are playing in my process of grieving. Oh my, the joys of womanhood and all our complexities. Now, where is that chocolate?

I would like to add what I heard almost every time I saw someone for the first time shortly after his death, and I know I surely would have heard it if I'd had a service for Chuck. I'd hear, "He's not really gone," that common statement made by well-meaning people trying to find a way to provide comfort, and they often tried so hard from the heart to help, but it drove me crazy! My blessing in life is that I realized deep down in my own heart that those awkward words and phrases are other's attempts at helping, but a little dark, sarcastic voice inside my head was screaming, "Are you effing kidding me? If he's not really gone, why do I not feel him or hear from him? He's really gone forever!" So, now I don't say anything to anyone else that has lost a loved one other than, "I'm here for you. Let me listen."

CHAPTER FOUR

---- WW ----

Support System
Did friends and family come to your aid?

TRISH

I was very blessed with a great support system of friends. Each one gave me their ears and hearts as well as thoughtful insight. It was important to get out of the house, especially in the beginning, and meet friends or family for a meal or coffee. I was also grateful for the take-out meals dropped off at my house, as this helped me adjust to being more comfortable in my home alone. None of my friends avoided contact with me. They all knew me well as a person that would greatly benefit from processing my grief with a well-trusted and objective friend.

I recall a terrible morning just as I was getting ready to shower when I threw a fit. Being alone in the house gave me permission to scream at the top of my lungs, cry out loud, and express my anger toward Bob for leaving this physical plane when he died. Within the following fifteen minutes, I received either phone calls or text messages from three friends asking me to meet that day. Their timing couldn't have been more perfect. I couldn't have been more blessed...truly my earth angels.

Since all but one of our relatives live in the Midwest, I can't say with certainty what their attitude toward me was. I kept in contact with Bob's sister, Ann, more regularly in the beginning because she was here with us during the week of his passing. Since she was the closer sibling to Bob, I knew it would be important to reach out to her more often. On the other hand, my sister, Allison, was a big support in ways she will probably never know. She, too, was here doing her best to keep my life on track.

PEGGY

Days after the celebration service, most friends and family went back to their own pressing lives. Soon, I was by myself much of the time. Friends and family members in town resumed their busy schedules. They were also dealing with Dan's loss and what that meant in their lives. Truthfully, I wanted and needed more attention from friends and family than they were able to give. I believed people were doing the best they could with their own busy lives, which were full of other responsibilities. I suspect the general thinking was that I was strong, capable, and able to handle this huge change just fine. I was grateful for what attention and help I did receive.

Eventually some friends did come spend days or a week with me. Several came from out of state. It felt very good to have people in the house day and night. I liked waking up to a house with people in it.

There was significant change in my attitude when friends

traveled to visit and stayed for a week or more. Thank you Linda, Elena, and John. My sister Rita has visited several times for two to four weeks at a time. Ahhh, it does my heart good. These close friends knew Dan, and they cared enough about him to come and be with me. I can't really explain the shift, but it was positive and I felt it.

Just the presence of a friend or family member was helpful because it made me feel like I was still significant, that I was worth visiting. I think that could be part of it. Part of the early days was recognizing I was still a person. Who am I now? I had been "Peggy & Dan" for over forty-two years. It was part of a necessary reset. When friends who'd known us as a couple for a long time visited, we didn't have to speak a lot about Dan being gone and the huge void that left for us. They just knew and I knew, and somehow that was very comforting to me.

One of Dan's close friends did confess to me two and a half to three years after Dan died that he'd avoided calling me because he would break down and become so distraught over Dan's death that he couldn't make the call. He said, "I think of you and Dan every day and sometimes I cry, because I miss my friend. I want to call you and I know it would be good for you if I called you, but I can't bring myself to do it." With empathy, I accepted his process of grieving. My process is not the only process going on here. As a person who had a lot of positive influence on many people, Dan's loss affected others deeply. They are all going through their own process of adjusting to his absence.

Dan worked out of town his last ten years. His workplace was a two-and-a-half-hour drive from home. Most of his co-workers were more his friends than my friends. They loved and appreciated him, and the feelings were mutual. I was very touched with the large number of his out-of-town friends who made the long drive the morning of the celebration service to show their love and respect and to support Dan's family. They offered sweet condolences, for which I am still grateful.

Since the day of the service, I have had only occasional contact via email with a few of Dan's coworkers. One friend said she had several dreams about Dan. She would email me and tell me about the dreams. That was nice. I received a couple emails during the first two years with messages like, "I just got a promotion using the skills Dan taught me and he would be happy. I just wanted you to know. His influence for good lives on." That warms my heart to this day.

Dan's family lives east of us by quite a bit. His eldest sister Pegi came for the celebration service. She and Dan's two other sisters have reached out and been in touch via phone and email.

JENNIFER

I have never been hurt so deeply and so profoundly in my life, but it is what it is, so I just move forward with what I have and look for acceptance and appreciation in all the wonderful people that did stick around to help us and support us. In the beginning, there were so many wonderful people willing and wanting to help me. As time went by, things changed, and just like any other time, people came and went out of my life. Such is the way of all things that change. I am again so very grateful to my girlfriends and their families that continue to love and support me and mine. I love them and would do anything for them anytime. And it's always good to keep likeminded company around because after a while, those that have no idea what you're going through will either leave you behind or unintentionally hurt you through their lack of understanding that grief isn't something that you just suck up.

Long lost friends from high school donated money that allowed me to hire a postpartum doula for six weeks. Nobody was going to nurture me after having a baby. Honestly, that alone is a topic for an entirely different book about the circumstances of giving birth. People came to sit with Chuck at the hospital and donated their time in energy and body work. Trish and her husband Bob were so gracious and compassionate when they gave Chuck body work treatments, called Reiki.

Food was delivered for months from friends I didn't even realize loved me so deeply, and then there was my midwife, Barb Pepper, a wise woman whom the universe chose to help me deliver Charlie Anne. At the time Miss Charlie Anne was discovered, I had gone back to the amazing woman who'd helped me deliver Hayden, but it turned out her son had a brain tumor and she wasn't going to be able to help with Charlie Anne's birth, and that's when Barb stepped in to take her place. Not only was she supportive, calm, and spiritually centered, but her experiences had also given her the abilities to be a death doula. There really isn't a lot of difference in the comings and goings in this world, as it's all uniquely challenging. It is because of Barb's amazing heart and soul that Charlie Anne didn't die and that Chuck died peacefully. I'm crying right now thinking of her and all that she's done for so many women. I'd like to be like her one day.

It was those moments that opened my eyes and heart to the depths of compassion that lies within us all. These are the miracles, and they are truly straight from God. Please don't ever take for granted the little things we do for one another, whether the person is a friend or a stranger, because these are not only gifts. They are the greatest miracles we will ever receive. I am so very grateful for my blessings.

My greatest source of hope has come from the Children's Grief Center here in town. I've been fortunate to be part of the support system because it has helped me bond with other young widows. I highly recommend going to grief centers when dealing with grief because it forces you to accept what's happening. It allows you to find healing if you're looking for it.

I haven't heard much from his relatives or friends since he died. It sucks when you think people will respond in ways you've heard in stories told to you by your great aunts and uncles and grandparents about the whole community coming together to help in times of great need. That just doesn't happen as often as it should anymore. I believe you can tell I'm still very disappointed by the abandonment. However, I don't understand what really happened here. Why did his family just leave our lives after his death, especially when Charlie Anne was just being born and Hayden was going to be without a father? I guess I can chalk it up to one of those everyone-grieves-in-their-own-way kind of things, but did they have to abandon me?

I have no idea how not to be bitter, and I believe y'all have gotten a good dose of my bitterness already, so I'll keep it short. My kids don't even recognize any of the names of Chuck's siblings or nieces or nephews. I guess I was expected to keep in touch with them, too. After all, it is a two-way street. I'll keep my bitter feelings to myself and instead apply the "Southern charm" I've come to understand as a very polite way of saying something nasty with a gracious, confusing smile.

It is what it is, so I just move forward with what I have and look for acceptance and appreciation from all the wonderful people that did stick around to help us and support us. As I said, I am so very grateful.

I'd like to add a different type of support system that I was and still am grateful for—the death benefits. Like most average adults starting their first family, I have little money, and I don't believe in having large amounts of debt, so Chuck and I either saved for the things we needed or splurged from time to time. Honestly, I don't think a life insurance policy of less than $500,000 is adequate enough for the average family to survive after the loss of the primary financial supporter. I am grateful that Chuck had little to no debt and neither did I, but having my income cut by more than two-thirds has left the three of us trapped in working poverty. However, I'm still doing my best to survive! I can only make so much a month or I lose my social security check and health insurance. I'm still trying to work out the details of how to be self-employed using my education in Ayurveda now that Charlie Anne is in school full time.

For those of you who have been or are single mothers, it's a true nightmare what our communities, or lack thereof, expect us to do to make ends meet. Therefore, I acknowledge that loneliness and financial sacrifice to be with my children is a blessing. It's been a tough road, but one I know I'm still learning to handle. I'm grateful for hearing the struggles and challenges of others so that I truly understand my blessings. Single parenting is messed up on so many levels. It's time to begin supporting local farming and small business so that we may have more opportunities to help and serve each other.

CHAPTER FIVE

Am I Losing My Mind?
Dealing with brain fog caused by grief

TRISH

Oh, the "brain fog." Due to the heightened state of emotional grieving, brain fog is likened to an actual weather fog. Memories just seem to get shrouded in a fog, making it difficult to remember the simplest of things. I've been told the brain fog that comes with grieving is likened to what cancer patients feel during their treatments.

I felt a great need to have some control and consistency in my life, especially in the beginning, due to my normal routines being turned upside down. However, I began to notice in the first few weeks after Bob passed on that I was becoming forgetful, thanks to my daughter pointing it out to me on numerous occasions. I had begun to feel embarrassed. Even though I felt fairly certain it was temporary, I didn't know how much time it was going to take for my ability to retain short-term memories to return. I decided to take action to keep myself on track and regain some control. I began using my calendar more often along with written to-do lists. I wasn't in a forced position of having to return to a 9-to-5 job, where I would need to depend on having a good memory. I made a conscious effort to try and find humor in my temporary state of forgetfulness and to find more humor in life. However, in the early months after Bob's passing, I did question if it was an age thing, but as time has gone on, and I'm finding more balance, my memory is returning. I still use the calendar on my phone and written lists. As a writer, this is very important because we aren't known for being the most organized-HA!

Using alcohol or other substances to cope...

I have never been a fan of alcohol in social situations or as a self-medication. I do not like how I feel if I have too much to drink, and I certainly do not like how I feel the next day. Occasionally, I like a beer or glass of wine, but that's the extent of my alcohol use. However, I have occasionally used cannabis medically to help me break through, release the heavy grieving emotions, and reach a state of clearer consciousness. Please do not mistake this for my advocating its use. Personally, it helped me to relax in the evening and sleep more soundly just as some would relax and sleep better after a glass of wine.

PEGGY

Brain fog! It's real! This was very frustrating. Ugh! Goodness! How did I go from being able to tackle many tasks competently and quickly to not being able to complete even one simple task without agony and frustration…and considerable tears?

Information did not register and stick in my mind. I could not remember two numbers in a row! I had to look at a string of numbers over and over again before I could get it right, copying one number at a time. Mama mía! I felt like most of my brain had been removed and the rest had been scrambled.

Extrovert is always how I was described. But with the brain fog, I felt like I was a trauma-induced introvert. My appetite for social settings suffered. Being in a crowd had become uncomfortable.

For most of my life I had a talent for knowing a face and name and being able to recognize the face and come up with the name even decades later. When the brain fog hit, I could not recognize the face and I surely didn't come up with the name. This was very embarrassing and awkward on many occasions. I had trouble tracking conversations. A person would tell me something, and a few seconds later I could not remember what had been said. It's possible some people thought I did not care about them or their conversation and felt offended, but I was doing the best I could at the time. I often asked a person to repeat the information.

The city street map that had been stored in my brain for decades was gone! Goodness! I had to rely on my car's navigation system to get to the grocery store, a girlfriend's house, and other places I'd driven to a thousand times. I couldn't drive without the navigation system. The maps just weren't in my head. I had difficulty using the GPS system on my phone because following instructions to learn the new system did not compute in my altered brain.

When doing office work, either personal or business, a ten-minute task would sometimes take me several hours. I would have to talk out loud to myself: "Now, reach for the stapler, grab the stapler, bring the stapler closer, now staple these pages, set them on the end of the desk, now open the file cabinet..." Really! It seems hard to believe, but that's what happened.

Out of necessity, I learned to talk aloud to myself, write lists, keep notebooks of conversations, have another person present, ask for help, and give myself space and time to make errors and to redo the project if necessary.

Death of a loved one can create a lot of work for the survivor. Dan owned a business, and I was faced with contacting many agencies and business offices. It was painful to have to explain over and over, "My husband passed away..." Ugh! Those were terrible first weeks, months, and years. I would often hear, "Call this number. It will be a ten-minute call." As it turned out, the call would take hours of run around. I would be transferred from department to department, which would necessitate telling my story over and over. This laborious process would just zap the energy right out of me. Sometimes I had to tell my story through tears, whether they knew it or not. I just had to keep going and pushing through. It took a lot of energy to maintain focus long enough to complete a task, which was exhausting.

It was imperative that I keep spiral notebooks that I filled with phone conversations and information I'd learned. I wasn't going to remember in ten minutes what went on during the conversations. There were many, many details to keep track of. Keeping notebooks, which I sometimes still do, was a huge help.

Not many people knew I was struggling with a thick layer of fog covering my memory and thinking abilities. I looked the same on the outside but on the inside, the nervous system and brain were struggling to adjust and reset the signals. Resetting takes lots of rest and a certain amount of time.

To move through brain fog, I first had to recognize it was real. Even though I felt a little crazy and had moments where I doubted my sanity, I soon came to realize I was experiencing something "normal." I tried to be patient with myself, but it was still very frustrating. I had some experience with brain fog when my sister experienced it after chemotherapy treatments. Perhaps what I went through was compounded by the fact that nine months before, when my friend died by suicide, I had begun to experience some brain fog. I didn't recognize it then. It got far worse when Dan died.

I learned to hire people to help me accomplish tasks. Sometimes I would ask a friend to be present with me in the room while I worked. There were times when the friend would do the talking on the phone while I quietly supplied information to her.

Ask for help! That is what I had to learn. I have a dear friend who comes over and helps me in my office. At times I've thought to myself, "Peggy, this is something you can do yourself." But it works a whole lot better with somebody else in the room.

Rest, time, patience, and healthy nourishment helped while moving through the fog. Something else that has been a big help is using certain essential oils or essential oil blends. I am grateful for the support I have received from these little gems of the earth.

In years one and three, I took continuing education

courses to maintain my license to practice massage therapy. In a couple classes, I was interested in the research explaining how the brain reacts to trauma. The nervous system sustains a huge mix-up in the way signals travel and fire certain responses. It takes time for the nervous system to "settle down" and begin firing normally again.

As you will read in the chapter titled "Self-Care," I did have moments where I doubted my sanity. I knew my thinking was very different from what I considered "normal" for me. This prompted me to visit a psychologist. This was an interesting experience. Whew! I learned I *wasn't* crazy after all, just adjusting to the shock and trauma of an unfortunate experience.

I have found it helpful to focus on music, comedy, healthy human connections, new adventures, good food, exercise, and supporting members of my business organization.

Walking around one of my favorite grocery stores offers familiarity and comfort. The environment is clean and cheerful, and the staff is friendly. I also found comfort and distraction in learning to play the ukulele and learning to draw using the Zentangle philosophy.

After Dan's service, when close family and friends gathered at our house, I made an announcement. "Please don't let Dan's death be the excuse for you to do something destructive." Meaning, let's face this like human beings who get to experience all kinds of emotions and let's move forward with healthy support.

Using alcohol or other substances to cope...

Rather than using substances to blur the pain, I allow

myself to feel it, to cry when I want or need to. Sometimes, as I moved along through my days, I could feel an intense sadness building inside. Crying would relieve the pressure, and I could move along again until the next episode. Eventually, the episodes happened fewer and farther between. To this day, the build-up of intense sadness still occurs, triggered by a multitude of factors. Over time and with healthy processing, the intensity of the pain diminishes.

JENNIFER

You may ask, "What on earth are you talking about?" Well honey, let me tell you. When you are grieving, you can't remember a dang thing. When the authors of this book and I sat down at a table to discuss our experiences and the endless possibilities of how to share them, I remembered—oddly enough on a topic about forgetting—how I thought I couldn't find my baby, Charlie Anne. Yes, I flat out thought I lost my brand new baby in my house.

I sat down on the sofa, crying. My sweet little Hayden came up to comfort me as little boys do when they see their sad momma. He asked what was wrong, so I told him I lost Charlie Anne, and he began to laugh so hard it confused me. Lo and behold, Charlie Anne had been wrapped to my chest and asleep the whole time. It was kind of like when you lose your glasses and they are on top of your head. We ate ice cream after that. There's nothing like something sweet for comfort and joy from time to time. And there's nothing like a little brain fog from time to time to keep you on your toes. All of us ladies had a good laugh over that shared experience. No one will ever be able understand the brain fog like us widows.

Using Alcohol or Other Substances to Cope...

Charlie Anne, my beautiful baby, needed me to be healthy so that she could be healthy, but I was still experiencing heavy bouts of anxiety, which by the way, can exacerbate brain fog. I don't think I handled the stress of it all too well, and every once in while I would smoke or eat marijuana—and yes, I have a legitimate medical marijuana card just in case you are wondering—to help deal with the horrible anxiety that I still experience with the same intensity today. However, today I typically eat the edibles because I don't ever want to be in a mental or emotional state where I can't be present for my children. There have been one or two times that I had too much to drink when they both were with my dear friends for a sleepover. Oh my! How on earth do some of you all do that every night? Hangovers are awful. Uh, no thank you!

CHAPTER SIX

I Miss You!
What we miss about our spouse in our everyday life. There are two comments we often hear regarding the loss of our spouse: "Well, you know he's not really gone" and "You know he's really still around you all the time." With those comments in mind, we also discuss the metaphysical presence of our husbands in this chapter.

TRISH

I held out right up to the end of Bob's life that he would just come back and be whole again. Every night I would pray for that miracle, and every day I would anticipate it happening, but I knew that was my "human" self wanting this. Over time, while he was in the ICU, I began to realize that my desire to have him back was what I wanted, but I had to ask myself if *he'd* want or need that. Eventually, I learned to accept the outcome. Time can heal all, but even though I believe this time-tested saying, I still miss him.

I'm sure, especially early on, what I didn't miss would

make a much shorter list. Bob was my rock, my best friend, my lover, my confidant, my journey partner, co-author of two of my manuscripts, co-founder and co-director of my North Campus Community Project nonprofit, father of our children, and a grandfather that was fondly called "Bobba."

I miss holding his hands and kissing his lips. I miss the feel of his skin. I really miss making love. I miss going to bed with him beside me and waking with him next to me in the morning. I miss listening to music with him. I miss his quick and zany sense of humor. I miss laughing with him over experiences that only he and I shared. I miss his strength when I was weak.

I miss camping with him under the stars. I miss watching how excited he got at a professional baseball or football game. I miss his master grilling skills. No one could make a juicier and tastier turkey on the charcoal Weber grill on Thanksgiving than him. I miss sharing a meal with him. I temporarily adopted a different location to eat dinner in the house because I missed him so much at the dining table. I miss my travel partner. We were never the obvious tourists. Tourists would often approach us for directions! We loved history and hanging with the locals to get to know them. We blended well wherever we traveled together.

I miss his mechanical and electronic skills. I miss his muscle around the house. I didn't realize how much I took his skills for granted until I needed them after he passed on.

I miss hours upon hours of spiritual talk over a pot of coffee in the morning. I miss our discussions in the evening with a couple of beers on the back deck about current events or ways we could help make the world a much better place. The deck is where the nonprofit was born and the draft of the two co-authored manuscripts written. I miss watching him tend the garden with our grandson Kade when he was just a little shaver. I'd look out from the kitchen window at the garden and see the two of them sharing ripe cherry tomatoes in delight. I miss watching the two get excited over their love of trains and train rides whether they were at the zoo or on the Rail Runner to Santa Fe for the day.

I miss watching our children sharing their achievements with him or asking him for his sage advice. It saddens me that our grandchildren will not have many—or worse, no—memories of their "Bobba."

I miss growing old with him. I miss having him here to fulfill and plan our second half of life together, a plan which was so abruptly cut short. I've begun creating new memories, not to replace the old, but to soften the things I so miss. Life is always changing, but it's all about how well one adapts to the changes and if one realizes they can choose how they move forward.

When we live with our spouse, we understand we are two people who love one another and are sharing a life together. However, just as in most relationships, Bob's and mine had its ups and downs, its challenges. A marriage is most often an ongoing process of growth and development. At times, I had difficulty seeing Bob in the highest light. Certain things irritated me, and some things he said really hurt me. I don't know if you ever get to a perfect relationship in a marriage, but when he left the physical plane, I was not only intensely sad, but angry we didn't have the opportunity to take our relationship to the next level. That was then…

Now I am grateful to have the natural ability to "talk" with Bob, and speak we do! Nearly every night after his passing, we would talk while I took meticulous notes about our conversations. He will even repeat things if I can't keep up with his dialogue! I would like to note that I could hear him talking to me in my mind. This is not unusual when two people are so energetically connected as Bob and I were. I noticed a pattern had emerged early on during these "conversations." He was now filled with unconditional love. Gone were his irritants that used to push my buttons. Gone were his reasons to be angry or disappointed with me at times. It was still Bob, but he was more than the sum of his earthly parts. He asked for my forgiveness in nearly every "talk" in the beginning, and when I asked him why, he replied, "Because I love you and I want to help your soul evolve in the physical plane you're in now."

Most of the time, I'm outdoors when this happens, but yes, on occasion, I speak out loud, though usually only when I'm inside the house because I don't want to hear from a neighbor, "Oh, that poor widow. She's really losing it!" Bob has really helped me accept his departure and has explained a great deal about why he departed, which has aided with my healing. What I love the most is the unconditional love that he shares with me now.

Engaging in activities my husband would have enjoyed...

On September 23, his birthday, I attended the Crosby, Stills and Nash concert with a neighbor because it was a favorite band of ours.

Seven months later, I had a meeting with a publisher in Los Angeles and I'd planned a trip to see a good friend,

Elizabeth Middleton, in Santa Barbara. I purposely decided to take the train from L.A. to Santa Barbara to reminisce about previous trips with Bob, and besides, we had always wanted to see more of the California coastline by train. I could feel him sitting beside me. I could feel his enjoyment. Across the aisle from me, there was a young, napping gentleman traveling solo, so I didn't pay much attention until he woke up, but when he did, I was shocked at how much he resembled Bob from when he was much younger! I kept passing brief glances at him as I extended my view out his window and found myself smiling from within. When I finally found my nerve to start a conversation with him, the illusion dissipated. His voice was so different than Bob's. Funny, how that works!

As time has gone on, I've done less of these things because as my favorite saying goes, "You can't drive forward while looking through the rearview mirror." I'm creating new memories!

Do I miss eating or preparing food with my husband?

I loved to cook when Bob was here. He enjoyed my cooking. I believe my cooking was what sealed the deal when we decided to marry! I was always trying new recipes between the standard dishes he most enjoyed, but now, I don't cook as often as I used to. However, if I indulge in a good beer or a good steak once in a while or another food I knew he enjoyed, I find myself asking if he enjoyed it, too! It's been three years now, and I don't find myself asking him nearly as often anymore.

Drawn to certain literature...

I never felt a need to read literature about the afterlife to help me understand his passing, nor did I engage with any inspirational books to aid in my healing.

Visiting places my husband enjoyed or was connected to...

Shortly after Bob passed on, I had an intense desire to visit Laguna Pueblo, a Native American Indian reservation forty-five miles west of Albuquerque, on their Feast Day in September. He spent nearly sixteen years as director of the Alcohol, Substance Abuse and Mental Health Program and considered his staff and the people of Laguna his extended family. On this Feast Day, and as I did nearly every year with Bob, I headed to Adele's, his administrative assistant's home, for the afternoon meal before heading to the plaza to watch the dances. Adele and her sister, Carmen, spotted me walking through the door and greeted me with a group hug as tears streamed down our faces. Bob's presence was palpable.

As I approached the kitchen table, I gravitated to my usual seat next to the head of the table that was always reserved for Bob, but this time, Adele insisted I sit in Bob's chair. I felt honored. Bob's presence was visceral. I could feel his enjoyment in the food as I ate. I've never been a fan of backbone stew no matter who makes it, but Bob always looked forward to indulging in backbone stew at Adele's every year at Feast time, so I found myself silently apologizing for not letting him indulge in his treat! Perhaps he found another way to indulge. On my way out to catch the dances,

Adele and Carmen invited me back next year. They may have been Bob's extended family, but in my heart, they were mine, too.

What would I do if I had one more day with my husband?

When I was writing this chapter, I was feeling very sad as I recalled what I missed about Bob and shed some tears. It had been a long writing day. It felt more like a marathon, to be exact. I grew tired after being on a roll, so I put away the laptop and went to bed. That night I actually had a full-on "visit" while on a different plane with Bob. I did not plan this visit, and it came without indication. I remained in a controlled state of lucidity at a time when most would consider it a sleep state because I was aware of my conscious thoughts as though I was awake and very aware of his departure and all the time that had passed. Our daughter Räna was there in the very beginning of the visit, and it warmed my heart to see the two hug. She departed after that brief moment.

I asked Bob to call our son Justin, and he did. Even though I was only a mere six feet away from Räna when they hugged, and Bob was on the phone with Justin, I couldn't hear their conversation. I could ask Bob questions, and he thoughtfully responded. His appearance was so soft and gentle. We hugged. I was so happy to finally see him and touch him.

I showed him around the house so he could see all the changes I had made. Of course, he said they were all very nice. I noticed he was different now. No critical judgment and very accepting. Gone was the familiar personality, and in its place was a new, loving man steeped in utter peace that I can't even begin to describe. One of the questions I had for him was, how I was going to explain this experience to others?

I took him into the walk-in closet we shared, pointed at the box on the floor, and asked him what he wanted me to do with his ashes, which I still had. After all, I still hadn't honored his wishes to spread them off the coast of Washington, as he had once expressed. He told me that wasn't important anymore. All of his responses were from a place of peace, love, and serenity, and all of his feelings toward me were of unconditional love.

I seized the opportunity, and I asked him if we could make love. He said yes without any change in emotion. I looked at the bed and actually apologized for replacing the king with a queen. Again, he was very accepting. It wasn't a typical lovemaking scene. It was a meshing of our unconditional love for one another in the highest sense. No foreplay, no orgasm, just pure feelings of love in a spiritual sense.

Here is a short excerpt of our conversation:

"...the more you can accept the present and move forward in your journey, those desires of the past (wishing he could be here with me) will change into new desires and the past will be in its proper place. Don't let your desires of what could have been rule over what can be. The sooner you can accept what was, the sooner you can achieve your new desires." He truly wants me to be happy.

"Loving me without conditions means you're forgiving me. That feels good. You're healing, baby, and I'm so proud of you," he said with such love in his voice.

I said in response, "I would appreciate a sign or

confirmation today that this was, indeed, real. You know me! I need proof. I love you, baby."

"And I love you, too, sweetie. Look for your sign."

After the "visit" concluded, I wrote the following words in my journal at 5:30 am on the deck with a strong cup of coffee:

Bob showed me what it's like to be present and accepting in each moment. No critical judgment...just love. Maybe this was a glimpse of his new world, a glimpse as to how I should strive to make my world here free of critical judgment and to live more in the present moment...how to live without conditions. I couldn't feel more grateful.

That experience had a profound effect on my life. I was shown two different scenarios of my life within twenty-four hours. The first scenario came during my writing marathon about how sad I was, how much I missed him, and how badly I wished to have him back here with me. The second was during our "visit," when he showed me how to be free of critical judgment through his examples of unconditional love and how to live in the present moment without conditions. Those examples have permeated every cell in my body. He was right, I had to let go of my attachment to the emotional ties from the past in order to move forward with my life so I can be truly open and receptive to good experiences and my desires. As I've said periodically throughout this book, you can't drive forward while looking in the rearview mirror!

And what about the sign? He sent it twice to make sure I got it! The single white butterfly to tell me it was time to fly on my own. *"Fly, baby! Fly!"*

PEGGY

On July 2, 2016, I was writing this portion of the book about what I miss. July 2 is our son, Kyle's, birthday. As I prepared to tackle this chapter, I found myself slipping into some very sad emotions, perhaps because this was the birthday of our firstborn, the child who made us parents, and I was really missing Dan. I didn't want to be alone while I wrote because I was concerned I would eventually start crying instead of writing. I called Trish, one of the other co-authors, and explained my situation. She understood completely, and this is the nice thing about having a friend in a similar situation. Trish came over and spent about forty-five minutes with me until I felt I could get back to telling my story and not feeling it all over again.

The answer to this question could fill a book. Dan and I were together all my adult life, for just over forty-two years. I miss different things about my life and partnership with Dan, depending on the day, the activity, or the occasion.

I miss having a confidant.

I miss the way he loved me; I knew I was the first one on his priority list. I'm no longer on the top of anybody's list. People are very kind when they offer to help me, but I know that I may wait days, weeks, or months until my task makes it into their busy calendars. This is just a fact of my new life. That's the way it needs to be because people have their own priority lists with someone else on top.

I miss Dan's generosity.

I miss holding his hand.

I miss making Dan laugh. I miss hearing his laughter. His laughter would sometimes involve his whole face and body. I loved that.

I miss the unspoken closeness and intimacy that we enjoyed. It developed over time and needed no words.

I miss being able to share insights with the person who shared most of my history and experiences. He was the person who understood what I was thinking by the look on my face, my body language, or just one spoken word. I miss sharing a laugh with the person who "gets it" because of a long, shared history.

I miss someone waking me up at three in the morning with an exciting idea that just couldn't wait for the sun to come up.

I miss having a partner who cares.

I miss my dance partner. Through the years, we developed our signature moves on the dance floor.

I miss having a companion and a play partner who knows what I like, and vice versa.

I miss taking road trips together.

I miss having a partner who cared for our children as much as I do.

I miss having a partner to share our grandchildren with.

I miss my partner, who cared about my siblings and knew everyone's history.

I miss the partner I worked beside for many years, raising our kids and planning for a happy retirement together. Retirement was only two years away. We looked forward to our "golden years" together.

I miss waking up Saturday morning and hearing, "Good morning, honey. What do you want to do today?"

I miss hearing Dan's voice. I am driving a car that Dan and I entered our contact lists into by stating the names and phone numbers, which the car's phone system recorded. I discovered, quite by accident, that I can still hear Dan's voice if I pronounce a name the way Dan entered it. It happened accidentally one day when I was calling my sister while driving. It startled me to hear his voice. I decided to have a good reaction to it and since then, when I want to hear his voice, I pronounce a name the way he did. Hearing his voice is music to my ears.

I miss being part of a couple. I seem to enjoy an experience more when I share it with someone I care about. Viewing a beautiful sunrise, sunset, or night sky is more enjoyable for me when I am sharing it. Also, it is interesting how life shifts in ways you never thought about. At times, couples are more comfortable with couples and don't think to include a solo person. I have been fortunate to have friends who do invite me to gatherings.

I miss being able to reach out and touch my partner. I miss the physical connection a lot.

While considering all I miss, I recognize I am grateful for what I *did* have with Dan. My gratitude list is long and I review that from time to time, sometimes daily.

Engaging in activities my husband would have enjoyed…

Dan and I enjoyed hiking and nature adventures. I still enjoy hiking and experiencing nature. This is a little tricky since I prefer not to go alone, especially on long hikes, and it seems we are all very busy these days and it is not often easy to find a friend who will join me. I still enjoy dancing, but not nearly as much as I did with Dan. I still enjoy visiting our children and attending their activities along with our grand-children's activities. Now, I've established activities of my own.

My new activities usually involve taking walks in a public park by myself or with a girlfriend, or some other activity like shopping, attending a concert or play, or traveling with a girlfriend.

As far as TV shows, I still enjoy some of the shows we used to watch together. We enjoyed watching *Dancing with the Stars* and *Last Man Standing*, both of which I introduced to Dan. I still enjoy these shows. For years I could hear in my mind the reaction Dan would have to what we were watching. Now I watch for my own enjoyment but still occasionally hear his laughter or comments in my head.

Listening to music is interesting. Sometimes it brings me joy and sometimes sadness. Sometimes I hear messages coming through music.

I consciously create new memories and try not to spend time trying to recreate the life I had with Dan.

Do I miss eating or preparing food with my husband?...

I think I have eaten more meat since Dan died than I did when he was alive. He was a meat eater, and I think in some subconscious way it's a little bit of a connection. I think I did that for a while, though not so much anymore because I'm not a big meat eater. There are times when I had a hamburger or a bite of steak or something because that was kind of a connection to something that he liked.

Dan enjoyed root beer floats. We often used root beer floats to celebrate with our sons. Dan delighted in teaching them how to create the perfect root beer float by pouring the root beer into the chilled mug and then ever so carefully introducing the scoops of vanilla ice cream into the sweet brown liquid. When the boys started making them for us, Dan would distract the float maker and when the boy looked away, Dan would gleefully poke the ice cream to the bottom of the mug and enjoy watching the boy rush to suck up the explosion of foam that was spilling out over the mug and onto the table. The boys and I have been known to enjoy a good root beer float in his honor when we get together or even when we are alone.

Dan was also fond of making a delicious green chile stew. Kyle posted Dan's recipe on the family website for cousins and friends. Whenever we make green chile stew, it is with Dan in mind.

Besides meat, Dan also enjoyed popcorn. I was not much of a popcorn eater or a meat eater while Dan was alive, but I find myself eating more of both since he died.

In 1976 Dan took a job in Tehran, Iran. We'd planned to stay for three years, but as the revolution heated up it became clear I needed to get Kyle back to the US. Eighteen months after we arrived in Iran, Kyle and I returned to the US. It was November. Dan followed six weeks later. We made many good friends while in Iran and fell in love with Persian food. To this day, when I eat Persian food, a part of me remembers our experiences in Iran. Pistachios are a link to the time our young family was enjoying a big adventure far from home.

For more than four years, I have been preparing good meals for myself like I used to cook for us. I use quality ingredients and lots of pots and pans. I make enough food for two or more people and make a pretty presentation. I spend a considerable amount of time cleaning up afterwards. I think that's about to change. I'm not sure exactly how, but rather than food preparation being a comfort, it is beginning to feel burdensome.

Cooking is one area of big adjustment in my single life. Cooking for one person is tricky. Serving good food is one of my love languages. It is just not the same when the only person I now serve is myself. It's now becoming more and more apparent that I'm eating for myself again.

Drawn to certain literature…

After Dan's death, I had a long list of recommended books to read for my business. Books I would have otherwise devoured, I could not bring myself to begin. This was not the time for me to read business-improvement and self-improvement books. I was on a mission to adjust to my new life and somehow recover a joy for living.

Especially in the beginning, I was attracted to three kinds of books: the metaphysical/ paranormal, which took me to the other side of the veil for experiences about people who had crossed over. The other type was autobiographies of people who were strong and overcame difficult situations in life, and the third was books about happiness.

I have read many, many books since Dan's departure. A few of the first books were *Saturday Night Widows* by Becky Aikman, *The Happiness Project* by Gretchen Rubin, and *Resilience* by Elizabeth Edwards.

I found it very helpful to tap into the minds of people who had an inkling as to how disconcerting it could be to lose someone, especially suddenly. It was also helpful to be aware of people who had more horrific experiences than me.

Some of the books I read were more for entertainment than for actual comfort. They were books I could read at bedtime that helped me fall asleep with a peaceful mind. I needed to read books that had something to do with a person adjusting to a significant loss or that had answers from the other side.

Visiting places my husband enjoyed or was connected to...

For several years, Dan enjoyed taking our family on Jeep adventures. One place we enjoyed visiting was Moab, UT. Since February 2012, I have driven through Moab on my way to Salt Lake City for a business conference several times. As I drive through the town, my mind plays a fast movie of the fun we had there.

We also enjoyed fun times in Durango, Colorado. At times when I'm in Durango, I feel I am enjoying it for the both of us.

What would I do if I had one more day with my husband?...

There's so much to cram into one day. I get emotional thinking about this question. If I could have him back physically for one day, I sure would have my arms wrapped around him until he faded away at the end of the twenty-four hours. I would do a lot of touching, I would do a lot of kissing, I would do a lot of looking into his eyes. I would tell him again and again, I love him. We did do a lot of that while he was alive, but, dang, I'd like to do it again!

In the early days after he left, there were questions that I would have asked him like, where is the insurance paper for this, or did you sign that? Would you call the state capital and close down your business so I don't have to deal with it for the next twelve months? What does this key unlock? Where is the key to the workbench?

Today, after spending over four years working through those issues, I would just bask in the glow of his presence. There would be a lot of people who would want to know he's back and want to spend time with him. I probably would keep him to myself. I'd call the boys and maybe my sister.

Beyond the hugging and kissing, if anything else intimate happened that would be great, but just being able to touch him and smell his cheek and neck would be wonderful. Any sort of exchange of love and love energy going and coming, and coming and going, I would love that! I wouldn't ask him to fix the compactor. I wouldn't ask him to listen to that funny noise in the car. I would just revel in his love and enjoy loving him. I would probably say something funny so I can hear him laugh again. I would soak up the sound of his voice.

JENNIFER

Death hurts like no other hurt, pure and simple, and oh my God, do I miss him. My bed is cold and my heart is broken. He's gone, taken away by illness, and he will never, ever touch me again. He'll never kiss our daughter. He'll never cook with Hayden again. He'll never do another thing in this world, never, ever again! I truly miss him.

Interesting thing is, I'm not sure if I really miss what our truth was on a soul level or if I miss what I've made up in my mind's eye to ease the pain. Either way, I miss him. I miss our long, wandering drives to find hole-in-the-wall restaurants to eat at. I miss his humor and his nonstop talking. I never thought in a million years I'd be with someone that talked more than me-HA! I miss that strong, protective masculine energy he had. I miss all the silly little gifts he was constantly buying for me despite my concern of overspending on unnecessary things. Most of all, I miss being snuggled up next to him at night. It's the hardest in the winter.

I have kept way too many of Chuck's clothes. Several in particular I kept because he had worn them and rehung them. They smell just like he did. I'd held onto one of his shirts so much while I cried through the night that I was afraid it had started to smell more like me than him, so I put his clothes in a zip lock bag for safe keeping.

On the other hand, I still wear some of his clothes. See, we always shared t-shirts and I always wore his "house pants," as he liked to call them. They were really pajama bottoms for men but they were always so comfortable, especially during the chocolate craving time. The difference is now I've cut the length off of them so they fit just me. I don't think he really needs them anymore. But then that does leave me wondering something.

You know how in the movies when people pass on they are often pictured in spirit wearing what they were wearing at the moment of their death? If that's true, there's no doubt in my mind Chuck's pissed about that because I let him be naked so he could be comfortable in the sheets. So, from time to time I wonder if that's why he's not coming around in spirit as much, because he's too modest to venture past the pearly gates in the buff. Oh, the joys of a highly active mind–HA! I don't sleep well, but I almost always have some form of entertainment going on in my mind. Why the hell can't it be way more comedy than horror or drama? Who could know, right?

I miss listening to music with him. I had to fast forward the Saturday Night Live featured musicians for years because I missed him so much, that even made me cry. Whew! It is said, "Time heals all wounds." Well, the way I see it, time helps you dry the tears and fills us with new experiences to react to. What's important is to try and react in the most positive way to each of the new experiences that life provides. I'm still learning how to do that.

Engaging in activities my husband would have enjoyed...

I love Chuck as much today as I did when we first met, but his hobbies were his and I enjoyed watching him do them. I'm slowly listening to a lot more music today, but don't ask me the names of any of the band members or if they've done projects with other musicians. I'd be hard pressed to answer that question. I pretty much can sing along with the ones I like, and that's it. Chuck was the historian and collector of music.

I'm starting to listen to his collection, and that's way more than plenty for me. I take great joy in listening to my kids sing hits from the sixties and seventies. Most kids their age don't have a clue about the power of that era's music. In my heart, I can feel he's smiling.

Speaking of Chuck smiling, he loved a lot of different types of music, and Black Sabbath was one of them. Well, it turned out they were playing their last concert, or so they were saying, in Albuquerque. I wanted Hayden to see and hear one of Chuck's favorite bands. It turned out Trish, one of the co-authors, wanted to see them as well since she had last seen them forty years ago in Chicago. It was a great concert! We had a blast singing the songs along with everyone else who was there to enjoy their last performance. Once again, I could feel Chuck smiling.

Remember when you went to a concert where you just *had* to have a t-shirt? I just *had* to buy Hayden one to commemorate the experience. And remember having to go out to a restaurant to have a late-night snack after a concert? With our best intentions to do so, reality struck quickly when Hayden, bless his heart, fell asleep in the back seat of Trish's car on our way to a restaurant.

Do I miss eating or preparing food with my husband?…

Oh my, how I miss his cooking and laughter. I never knew how punishing silence could be until he was gone. That man was a bull in a china shop. The sounds of pots and pans crashing in the kitchen at odd hours of the night is gone. I still wake up wondering why the house is quiet even though I know why, and today I just sigh a little, missing the smell of baked delicacies.

I don't bake like he did. He was a master at baking. I was a master at eating it. Chuck was also very much a homebody. I'm hoping that one of my children, most likely Miss Charlie Anne, will bake. I miss him waking me up in the early morning hours to taste test whatever dessert recipe he'd been working on. Thank the good Lord, I can still indulge once in a while on the chocolates Chuck loved to bake, not because I can bake them, but because I can always find a bakery or a great dessert somewhere.

I have, on occasion or two, tried to recreate something he made, but again, in all honesty, what he baked was more often than not horribly rich and fattening. Since I'm single now and I want to have sex, watching my weight is more important to me. Maybe I'm sharing way too much information here, but I'm hoping you all will be curious about my thoughts on the subject of sex in the chapter, "Sex and the Reluctant Single Woman." I don't hold much back.

I miss the way he was always happy to cook for me and feed me, and for that matter, anyone that crossed his path. I look in my refrigerator and can't tell you if we have things to eat, where he could open the fridge with it looking truly empty and come out with some fabulous entree. Yeah, we're starving a lot more often without him here—figuratively speaking, of course. I don't grill but have been informed by my son, who still remembers Chuck firing up the little pit, that we will be doing just that this summer. Ah, new beginnings.

Visiting places my husband enjoyed or was connected to...

Thank the good Lord driving is easier than baking. I take my kids to the places Chuck and I ate at or lived. I take them to visit friends of his when they're willing to see us. Traveling is an easy way for me to share with my children some of the things he and I did.

What would I do if I had one more day with my husband?...

There's no doubt I'd jump into his arms with desire and longing and then I'd flip out on him for not going to the damn doctor two years earlier, when the pain started. Then after my tongue lashing I would curl up in his arms to cry, knowing he'd be gone again. My heart and soul miss all of him so deeply. I just cry when these moments of missing him come around. They have yet to go away. I'm just given more opportunities to fill in the empty space that will always be his.

CHAPTER SEVEN

Messages From Him
Due to our close relationship with our spouse as well as our ability to tune in to our intuition, we feel, at times, that we are receiving messages from our deceased loved ones.

TRISH

I've had two dreams, albeit both were very brief. In one, I saw him standing at the end of the bed dressed in a suit and looking at me as I entered the walk-in closet. The second was a little more interesting. In the dream, it was nighttime and I saw Bob lying in the bed next to me and looking at me very serenely. As I sat up on my left elbow for a better look, what surprised me was seeing another soul mate standing in front of the armoire, looking at me. As soon as I looked back at my husband, Bob had vanished, ending the dream. Hmmm…

I'm a skeptic about psychic mediums giving messages to people that long to hear from a loved one on the "other side." Last fall my co-author for this book, Peggy, invited me to her home with nine others to see Robert Baca, a psychic medium for Voices From Heaven (voicesfromheaven.com). It took a couple of phone calls for Peggy to convince me to attend due to my skepticism. Finally, I thought, "Why not?" I politely accepted. I knew I would be able to detect a fraud a mile away. However, just a couple of days before attending, while Bob and I were conversing as I transcribed our conversation, I told him to send me a sign that what he'd said about how sorry he was for putting me through so much and to please continue working on forgiving him was real during the upcoming event.

Just as Robert Baca was about to take a break, he said, "Bob? Robert?" I sat back down and told him that message may be for me. Immediately, my Bob went into how sorry he was for all he had put me through and revealed details about our conversation just a few days before. He said he'd been there to greet my father when he passed over. What really surprised me was when, through the medium, he said how much he'd loved watching the balloons being released during the Celebration of Life we had for him. Robert Baca had no clues beforehand about my circumstances or any details about me personally. I must say, I was impressed with his ability. I, too, was relieved to know I wasn't a nut-case after all and that I could truly communicate with Bob. See? I really am a hard-line skeptic!

Animal Messengers…

One evening while I was sitting on the deck within a couple of weeks after he passed on, a raccoon sat up on an embankment above the pond and stared at me. Even though I had a very strong sense it was Bob, the mere sight of an actual raccoon spooked me so that I ran into the house. Sorry, Bob!

Since then, there have been so many raccoons causing havoc in the pond. I guess they got my number-HA!

Do insects count? Long before Bob left this physical plane, we would quite often see two small, white butterflies flutter about in the low lying vines around our deck. He would say, "That's us, baby." After he left this physical plane, I would often be reminded of his departure because I would only see one small butterfly fluttering about. I grew to understand the single butterfly represents me in this present time.

He sends me bird feathers as his reminder he's with me. Most often they will just gently flutter to the ground directly in front of me. One day when I finished loading my groceries in the car with the windows rolled up, I closed the back hatch and sat down in the driver's seat. When I looked at the passenger seat, I noticed a six-inch, beautiful white feather laying there. I knew immediately that it was a message from Bob, that he was saying he was with me. There's something very comforting about his messages.

Recently, I had another breakthrough in my growth and development. While writing in my journal on the deck in the early morning, I caught a glance out of the corner of my eye of my spirit totem, the dragonfly, gently clinging to a pond reed fluttering in the breeze. The wings reflected a brilliant gold color from the rising sun. I knew immediately this was a message from my higher self reminding me of the healing and transformation I'm experiencing. I couldn't help but smile, and gratitude poured forth. Later in the day, the dragonfly returned, but this time he brought along a friend, a hawk, that was perched in my neighbor's tall tree just feet away from me. The hawk was a dominant spirit totem of Bob's. I couldn't have been more blessed!

PEGGY

Dan's metaphysical presence is comforting, but it does not warm my toes on cold nights and it does not dance me across the kitchen floor when good music comes on.

Spiritually, I still feel very connected to him. In the early days after Dan's death especially, I could have supplied his responses to conversations or situations. I could have done this partly because I had experienced a lot of life with him and knew how he responded to most situations and partly because I have trained myself to listen to my inner thoughts and intuition.

I do talk to Dan aloud. Most of the time I am alone in the house with my memories and an energetic connection to him. Sometimes my conversation with him begins with a question like, "Dan, where is the paperwork I need to send to so-and-so?" I listen for inspiration. Sometimes I'll share some news we wondered about while Dan was alive: "Dan! I found out why the neighbor got sick!" Sometimes I'll speak about concerns I have with the boys: "Dan, offer him some guidance on this issue."

Sometimes when I come home from an out-of-town trip, I will walk into the house and call his name. It just makes me feel good to pretend for a moment. "Dan, I'm home!"

I also feel at times like I can hear him talking to me. When a person dies, the physical presence goes away, but the energetic connection can remain strong.

In the beginning I spoke to him a lot out loud, in my head, and in my journal. One question I'd ask was, "You really thought it was okay to leave now? The way you did?"

Most nights I sleep well once I get really tired and fall asleep, but sometimes I'll wake up early in the morning feeling like a message is coming through. I grab my journal and start writing. I'll write down thoughts that are moving quickly through my mind. When the message ends, I put the book away and go back to sleep. I don't look at the writing for a week or two, sometimes longer. When I do read the journal entry, I am surprised. The message sounds like Dan talking. That has been nice.

It has been at least six months since the last journal message. Toward the middle of the fourth year, I was not as quick to journal all the conversations I intuited. It seemed I did not need them as much as I did in the beginning. I still enjoy when I perceive a message and I listen to it, but I do not always record it.

In the five years since Dan died, I have had dreams about him that were nurturing and supportive. I wake up with a smile on my face and a feeling of peace.

Sometimes I hear his response to a situation in my head. Perhaps that is because I knew him well for a long time and was accustomed to hearing his responses so now my imagination fills in the blanks.

I also find pennies in the oddest places. Dan and I had a joke about pennies from heaven.

One Saturday morning when we were taking a walk, I found a penny. I said, "Mom says found coins are God's way of paying a housewife." In her day there were many women who dedicated their time and energy to the rearing of children and keeping a happy home…with no paycheck. A few moments later I found a nickel. Dan's quick comment was, "Look, you got a raise!" I connect found pennies and other coins with Dan's presence.

Sometimes I have asked for a sign that Dan is metaphysically present. One morning as I was getting in my car to head to a meeting, I was really missing Dan. I asked him to let me know he was near. As I was backing out of the garage, the radio DJ was commenting on the last song. The next song to come on was a song Dan introduced me to when we got married: "Call me Irresponsible" by Jack Jones. That felt like confirmation that he was near. The meeting I went to lasted several hours. As I got into my car after the meeting, I changed the radio station and the song that came on once again was "Call Me Irresponsible" by Jack Jones!

Interestingly, there have been times when I was talking in my head or aloud to Dan and an object flew off a shelf with no visible help. One time a bottle of wine shot straight out of the wine rack then fell and shattered on the tile floor of the kitchen.

I keep a journal about interesting incidents. At times when I journal it seems some messages become even more clear. Yes, I feel out-of-the-ordinary situations offer support and comfort. There is a peaceful feeling that lingers.

I've had a handful of dreams over time. I wake up from the dreams and feel like I really have been with him. I feel happy and at peace. After reading one of his books on communicating with loved ones who have passed on, I scheduled a reading with medium Patrick Mathews (patrickmathews. com). I waited six months for the date of my reading to arrive because Patrick has quite a following. At one point he seemed embarrassed to continue with the thought that was coming through. "Gosh, I've never gotten this before, but… does he come to you in dreams?" Patrick was choosing his words and stumbling a little. "Uh, have you made love in your dreams?" A few days later I did have a dream like that. It was just sweet, really sweet. I think that was the last dream I had with him, and that's been months ago. That's a nice last dream, if that ends up being the last dream I have of him.

A few times, mostly at night or in the early morning, I have been awakened by Dan calling my name. I answered him and then realized he was not physically here because I was alone in the house. I felt certain I'd heard his voice with my ears, not just in my mind. It is odd, and I cannot explain it.

I've had several readings with professional psychics. Some of my favorites are Betsy Morgan-Coffman, Robert Baca of Voices from Heaven (voicesfromheaven.com), Patrick Mathews, and Roy Worley of Mystical Ship.

All messages have been amazingly accurate and specific. There is comfort in the messages. They are a confirmation of thoughts or intuitions I have experienced previously.

Animal Messengers...

About a month after Dan's death, I was sitting quietly outside, contemplating. My thought was, "What's your sign going to be for me?" Two beautiful butterflies flew very close to me and danced around for a moment. As they disappeared, two hummingbirds flew very close to me and played with each other before they flew out of sight. The animal messengers have been a comfort. Somehow, hummingbirds and butterflies became symbols of his love being present.

JENNIFER

I'd thought by now Chuck would have given me a few more profound signs. Honestly, I think I'm just too dang tired from years of constant stress to be receptive to any of his signs. However, I've had two dreams that were more along the lines of origin stories related to the circumstances of this lifetime's story with Chuck while he was still alive. Twice, I've had an intuitive person say something to me about him, but he never was the one sending the message. He was once only a facilitator for my mother's message to me after she'd passed. Yeah, again, I'm too dang tired to figure that out just yet. So, I'll wait and hope that those long-gone teenage years of abundant sleep will one day return. It would be a time where I will be allowed, at the very least, to get enough sleep to receive more messages.

I do try and listen for any messages from Chuck until I clear my mind or fall asleep. As you've guessed, I hardly ever sleep. It's tricky trying to clear one's thoughts on good days. Try doing that through years of thinking, "Holy shit! This is my life now!" So I'd say out of the nearly seven years, I've truly tried listening twice—during those rare moments where the kids were gone and my belly full of healthy, good food, leaving me with hours of free time to catch that monkey running around in my brain that's always escaping.

I really wanted a message, a dialogue, or even a moment of comfort from Chuck in that first year he was gone, but instead, I was screaming hysterically like an arguing couple on the front porch in the early morning hours. I can almost guarantee that if your neighbors are sympathetic, they won't call the law on you, and on a rare occasion, may even offer a meal or handpicked vegetables or flowers from their garden.

Here is an example of a late night, single-sided conversation. I'd screamed, "How could you do this to me?" And I don't always say it quite so nicely. It's not like he's going to fight or argue with me. I might as well speak my mind. I always ended up telling him how much I miss him, but there were times I wanted to know how his journey is going. There's still no response. He didn't care about spirituality and what lies beyond the physical plane. It kind of pisses me off that he's in the "knowing" and he's still not giving up any of its secrets. He's still teasing me from the beyond. Yeah, I think he's a jack ass from time to time. However, that was the fun of our relationship. We almost always could laugh at how absurd our arguments could get. I miss that, too.

I don't really believe in the whole heaven or hell thing despite my very dedicated Methodist upbringing. I'm faithful about the ideas of Jesus and his teachings, but then I learned over the years from the beautiful teachings of many other great sages during my short lifetime that fear and punishment, just like heaven and hell, is a state of mind. Therefore, my traditional upbringing conflicts with my new understanding of spirituality. Since my mind is more open to new ideas, I became intrigued by stories about near death experiences that could possibly give me a glimpse of where Chuck went after he died.

It wasn't like I had enough going on when Chuck died, but to add to it all, I had to deal with passing comments from those who believed in well-meaning, fear-based faiths. I had to take a closer look at those stories about near death experiences to help me deal with Chuck leaving this physical plane. I had to find some kind of anything to help me understand that

Chuck wasn't going to be damned to hell for an eternity. Oh, those old rooted beliefs needed to be put to rest.

To my relief, due to the commonality of near death experiences combined with the writings and prophecies—yeah, I know, watch out for the false prophets—of Edgar Cayce along with Buddhist, Taoist, and Hindu teachings and a bit of my own faith-based upbringing, I've now come to understand that we all go on a continued journey of spiritual evolution into many realms of ever more levels of pure love. If that dang little monkey playing around in my mind would just stop playing with doubt and fear, I very well could become a sage. Haha! High hopes, baby. You've got to have high hopes to manifest a great dream like that.

I did one time go to a psychic here in town. He was an amazing man whose name I can't seem to recall or I'd give recognition to him right now. As I look back into my memories, I recall him having conversations with forces I could not see. He was in a heated conversation with Chuck about his spiritual evolution. According to the psychic, Chuck did not want to leave this physical plane because he wanted to be here for me and our kids, even though Miss Charlie hadn't been born yet.

I have come to believe he talks to me through this electrical universe with music. When I ask for a message, I've learned to ask for a song that I definitely can remember or associate with him. This method of communication with Chuck began when I went to pick up his ashes from the funeral home. After all was said and done inside, I went to the car sobbing. I turned my radio on and heard dead air. That seemed an appropriate term for the experience I was having. There is nothing like sitting with the remains of a six-foot-two man in your lap packaged in a container the size of a shoe box.

I took a deep breath and begged Chuck for a sign. I backed my car up with silence on the radio. As I began heading home, the most appropriate song came on—Blue Oyster Cult's, "(Don't fear) The Reaper." At least now I was crying with a smile. That's when my faith of communicating with him first began. Sometimes I hear a song when I ask, and sometimes I hear a song when I've forgotten I've asked.

I've had two dreams with him in it, but they had nothing to do with the life we'd had. I think the dreams contained a message about karma and featured at least two past lives we've had, neither of which seemed very happy. In these dreams, it's clear that he's a strong-willed man in all of his lives whereas in my past lives, it's clear I never have been one to change someone, take 'em or leave 'em, because I believe people only change when they really, really need to or want to. From what I've observed in my short lifetime, most people don't change that much and most people aren't even willing to change.

Both the dreams I had involved him being a very powerful man within a community. In both dreams, I wasn't as significant to him as I was in this lifetime. I'd like to believe in this lifetime we finally came to an understanding of love between each other. I'm also guessing that maybe he left early so he could feel just how much he really loved and needed me. Cancer left him completely dependent on me for so many things that he never thought he'd need. I'm grateful I had those last weeks to really learn how to love him unconditionally and start me on the path to forgiving him for leaving us. I feel in his last weeks here in this physical plane, he was able to feel the gift of unconditional love from me.

CHAPTER EIGHT

Help! I Can't Do This Alone

How we came to realize we were not only learning to live without our husbands but also learning to accept the new need to call on others for help. After family and friends return to their own busy lives, the beautiful condolence flowers wither and dry up, and we find we are alone... what then? We spend a lot of time and effort learning to live together and then we spend a lot of time learning to live without the other.

TRISH

In our marriage, I was the one who handled the finances, Bob handled the car, and we both handled the home repairs/maintenance according to our individual or combined skill level. For example, I didn't dare try and grill and would only assist when called upon, while he didn't feel comfortable in the kitchen unless he was making coffee, a sandwich, or carving a grilled meat. I guess you could say we had definite territorial boundaries, but it worked for us. While he was grilling, I was putting together the side dishes. I learned after he passed that I had taken for granted the things he was better at doing than me.

Since Bob passed away in the summer, it took me several weeks to realize the lawn needed mowing and that I wouldn't be able to start the old thirty-something-year-old lawnmower as Bob could. One would assume that since I'd founded a nonprofit that emphasizes helping our neighbors in need that I would find it easy to reach out for help in *my* time of need. No! It wasn't easy at all! I didn't want to burden the kids early on. I knew they were processing their dad's passing, and I wanted to appear strong for them. Also, I could sense the kids felt very uncomfortable being in the house where all their memories of us as a family resided.

One day my doorbell rang and two of my wonderful and generous nonprofit volunteer neighbors, John and Betsy, whom I had grown very fond of since the start of our nonprofit, asked if they could mow my grass. I wanted to say yes, but I felt very awkward being on the receiving end of help. I reluctantly agreed once they reminded me it's a two-way street. I was the neighbor in need, and it was time to reap what I had sown. What a lesson in learning to be a gracious receiver as well as a gracious giver. In that moment, I was truly living in harmony and balance. I really considered John and Betsy to be my earth angels.

Regarding the vehicles, I am fortunate my son-in-law, Leo, owns a car dealership with mechanics on site, so that was an easy and very grateful transition. Leo is so busy with his car business and his recently expanded family, my new grandson, that I do my best not to ask him for his help regarding the repairs around the house. The home repair contractors I find are usually selected from a reliable referral.

We each had our own strengths, and because of Bob's absence, I had to realize early on that all was in divine order and if things didn't get done, they would eventually. I had faith that I would be guided to ask the right person for help or someone would just show up in my life, as my neighbors did when they asked if they could mow the grass. I will say that over time, I have grown to be more accepting of the things I can't do, and yet, I have had to learn to do things I never thought I would.

I recall when Bob suggested I learn how to use the Xbox for watching movies. I told him if he passed away before me, I would just get rid of all the electronic equipment. It was that simple, or so I thought. I had a natural resistance to certain devices, and after all, I had an electronic wizard for a husband! You know, it was one of those division of tasks. Well, when he did pass on, I realized I had a greater desire to watch DVDs to fill the void created from no longer being able to have wonderful evening conversations, and I *had* to learn how to operate the equipment. In other words, I had to eat my words. I'm sure Bob was laughing at me. Now I look like a pro…well, sort of.

During one of our intense spring winds in New Mexico, a thin but mighty branch snapped from one of the elms around the deck and took a portion of the table umbrella down with it. The branch came to its final resting place across the pond. The white lights under the umbrella had burned out when the umbrella became damaged. After assessing the situation, I thought it would be a good idea to replace some of the strands of miniature white lights that had burned out on the coyote fence surrounding the deck.

See, since Bob was the electrical wizard, he'd found a way to connect the lights on the coyote fence with those under the umbrella so they would light up all at once with a remote control from within the house. Replacing the umbrella and all those strands of lights would have been a task Bob and I would have tackled together with me as his assistant, of course. It would have been completed in just a mere few hours. But no! I called around to see if I could get some help, but no knight in shining armor came to the damsel's distress call. I gave up waiting after a few weeks and decided I was smart enough to figure out how to connect all the strands of lights and strong enough to handle a ten-foot umbrella on my own. Just as in the old story about the Little Red Hen when no one came to her aid and she said, "Then I will!"

And I did! It took nearly a whole day with a couple of reassessment breaks over an ice tea to accomplish this, but the feeling of confidence and pride that I could still handle a job independently as well as the feeling of success from learning a new skill filled me with satisfaction!

Later, I ended up buying a lightweight cordless recharge-able weed whacker that I can handle more easily and hired someone to mow my lawn. I'm still contemplating purchasing a battery operated lawn mower just as a matter of convenience.

Slowly but surely and day by day, I am growing into a new role as a single person. I could have chosen to lament over my new situation, but I decided it's healthier and it feels better to embrace the present because the past is just what it is…in the past, and this is now!

Feeling vulnerable…

I felt safe with Bob. Once he was gone, there seemed to be a few more creaks in the night than I recalled, and it made me feel vulnerable. I decided to be more proactive and upgraded the security system. Since I'm an animal lover, I thought briefly about getting another dog, but I knew if I did, one of my two cats would bring new meaning to having a "hissy fit!" Over time, I became more accustomed to being alone.

PEGGY

I've taken on all this new work and I've completed innumerable new tasks and he's still dead! That was a thought that hit me one day after tackling a long list of tasks. I knew tears and accomplishments would not bring him back. I knew I needed to establish a network of people I trusted to help me with a variety of aspects of my new life. I needed help!

Oh my goodness, there is a lot of work to do when thrust into the role of widow. I had meetings with our attorney, Dan's certified public accountant, my bookkeeper, our insurance agents, plumbers, electricians, security company reps, and bankers, among others. I was running my own business and closing down Dan's. I was dealing with the state representatives, paying taxes, still moving into our new house, selling Dan's truck, and maintaining my vehicle. I was on the phone for long hours trying to get records straightened out and changing accounts into my name. I was dealing with insurance companies, which took far more hours than one would guess. It was difficult to tell "my story" over and over each time I was transferred to another department or agent. The amount of details needing attention was overwhelming, but I persevered. I enlisted the help of a sister-in-law and a friend. This help was necessary because not only was the number of tasks overwhelming, but I was in the grips of the shock and brain fog that accompany a sudden trauma and change in one's life.

So after days, weeks, months, and years of facing challenges and meeting with success accomplishing previously foreign tasks, I was still alone! All that work hadn't changed the fact that my beloved partner is still gone, and I have more alone days and innumerable tasks ahead. It's so very disappointing but true. Bummer!

Since the age of eighteen and a half, Dan was the main character in my life. He was my protector. He was my buffer to the world. He was larger than me, strong, capable, and resourceful. We leaned on each other for help in minor situations and major situations. This became especially noticeable when he was gone.

In a partnership, each person eventually gravitates to the tasks they are comfortable with, which leads to a natural and comfortable division of labor.

I am almost amused when I think back to the early days after Dan's death. I thought I would keep moving through life like Dan and I had been. I tried to take over the household, yard, and financial tasks that he had typically taken care of along with all in my bailiwick. I tried doing it all.

It was easy to feel overwhelmed with the big life Dan and I had created. I knew I could not handle it alone, but I did all I could on my own. Eventually, I realized I needed help. People kept asking if my sons were coming to help me. I felt the boys were the first people I would want to come help, but I understood they had busy lives and two out of three lived out of town. Most importantly, they were dealing with their own grief. They did what they could, but the job was huge and I learned to walk past the piles of boxes or items begging to be dealt with. I learned to have peace amongst the chaos.

Kyle makes himself available whenever he can, and I always appreciate his help. He troubleshoots technical issues for me on the phone or in person. Kyle has a mind and attention to detail like his dad. I trust him to do a project right the first time. It is a great comfort to have him nearby, only ten minutes away by car.

Brother Dan was helpful in the beginning. I think coming to the house where his best friend died became too much for him, and he no longer offers his assistance.

Sister-in-law Jennifer was a tremendous help with paperwork in the early days. I unreservedly trust her with my personal information, and it was a great comfort to have her by my side as I began to negotiate innumerable important tasks.

Noah and his wife, Stephanie, met and married several years after Dan died. They make trips once or twice a year to visit me. Sometimes I visit them. Being together and sharing good times is nice and necessary. They do what they can to help when they come for a visit.

Birk was serving in the US Navy when Dan passed away. He had several more years to serve. He is back to civilian life now, and a few months ago he drove over a thousand miles to come help me pare down some of the items in my garage. Birk took all his tools and his huge tool box that we housed for him when he enlisted. He also took many of Dan's tools that I have no use for and made sure I kept plenty of tools to maintain my property. This was a tremendous help.

Debi and I have shared a friendship for over twenty years. She read books about widowhood so she could better understand what I was experiencing. She also made herself available to just be with me. She spent hours with me in my office, working through details of my new responsibilities as sole owner of my business, vice president of Dan's business, and owner of a new house. Her help has been indispensable.

From time to time, I will receive a surprise text from dear friends who lead very busy lives traveling the world as owners of dōTERRA International, the company I am gratefully involved with. The texts express love and caring and are a huge pick-me-up.

John Lowe, owner of Panorama Homes, builder of our new home, has been a good member of my support team. He and his staff, especially Carol and Michele, have been responsive to my needs. I am most appreciative of their help.

I tried keeping the yard neat and tidy until one day, about two years in, I decided it was all right to hire someone to help with the yard. I think I was getting comfortable with being the sole bread winner *and* spender in the family. Heck! I *was* the family. All decisions were now up to me, so I decided to pay for a landscape-maintenance helper.

In the first year AD (After Dan), I hired a professional window cleaner. I was timid about doing this. It goes back to feeling vulnerable and being cautious about inviting people into my space. I called a window cleaner recommended by a girlfriend and made sure she was with me when he arrived. I felt that clean windows might help improve my attitude. I was willing to try anything to stay positive about life. It turns out this window washer is a very honorable person and I feel completely comfortable with him.

My crew, or posse, has come together over time. To date, I have hired a window washer, a landscape maintenance helper, plumbers, tile crew, an organizer, an electrician, a bookkeeper, a CPA, financial advisors, and a few other helpers. Sons and friends have helped from time to time. Of course, any and all help is greatly appreciated but not expected.

We live in a world in which most people are living busy lives. I haven't found one person yet who has so little going on that he has jumped at the chance to make me number one on his list. Nope! That ended with Dan's death. That was a sobering realization. I was no longer number one on anyone's list. My needs would come when and if someone could fit them in on their schedule, not mine. Part of the new reality I was adjusting to.

To accommodate my new life, I purchased a leaf blower that fit me better than Dan's big blower did. I purchased tools that would help me take care of the house and yard rather than use the heavier, larger tools that fit Dan and filled the garage. I even purchased a screwdriver that was pretty with a flower print on the handle.

Dan was quite a skilled, resourceful, and willing handyman. Over time, I had to figure out new ways to take care of the never-ending to-do lists that come with homeownership. That usually involves paying someone, so every time I turn around I'm paying someone to help me with something. It gets the job done.

Feeling vulnerable...

In the beginning I felt very vulnerable and overwhelmed. Part of the value of writing this book with other widows is that we could get together and laugh and cry and understand each other. We are good support for each other. It is helpful to spend some time with other widows. Be selective, find widows you fit with. You may not resonate with all widows because experiences are different, partnerships are different, and circumstances are different. Unfortunately, there are plenty of widows to choose from.

Here I was in a newly built house, alone, listening to the creaks and groans of new construction as it settled. There seemed to be lots of little noises that got my attention at night. I wasn't fearful; I just thought perhaps I needed to be aware of the sounds in case I needed to fix something or explain to someone what I'd heard.

As the reality of being totally responsible for myself, my well-being, and safety settled in, I developed some interesting new habits. For example, I purchased a lot of flashlight-type gadgets. Did I not want to be in the dark? I put flashlights and night lights all over the house. We had installed the top-down, bottom-up blinds in the new house. In the early months and years, during the times I felt more vulnerable, I opened the blinds just enough so that I could see out but people could not see in. I didn't want to be on display or easily seen, I guess. I just felt better being in my protective cocoon.

JENNIFER

Now here's where it gets fun, because when Chuck was dying and shortly thereafter, it's fairly obvious, even to those that don't quite get it yet that you're probably going to need some help doing the "manly" things. My neighbor across the street from the house we lived in mowed the lawn. Others' husbands or partners came and did minor repairs that you married women take for granted, myself included. Then time enough passes, and everyone is quickly back to their own thing and I'm alone with small children.

Hayden was too young to understand that I couldn't fix a highly technical toy because I was sleep deprived while caring for his new baby sister. There's a lot of stuff I've gotten rid of because I didn't have the capacity or ability to concentrate long enough to figure out how to use or fix it. That's when I slowly began to learn that I had to do as much as I can alone or pay someone to do it for me. That stuff gets expensive, but hey, I can unclog my tub from the massive amounts of hair, unclog my toilet from the massive amounts of toilet paper, and I can climb on my roof to turn my swamp cooler on. Hell yeah!

Chuck did what he was good at. I did what I was good at. It always balanced out. Now that he's gone, I realize how horribly lacking my meal planning skills truly are. I might as well throw in the towel when it comes to my housekeeping abilities and parental guidance because I definitely feel under qualified to be placed in multiple generational roles such as mother, father, aunt, uncle, and let's just throw in grandparenting as well, because in our lives, it's just us three. Women are supposed to do it all regardless of the situation thanks to today's idiotic ideology about a woman's role in society. I want to live as an elephant in a well-established matriarchal clan of understanding and compassion, or at least that's what my fairy tale day dreaming mind would like.

Here's one of those examples of a miracle, at least when we truly listen, and in my case I had completely surrendered listening. A dear friend of mine, after patiently listening to my hysteria, said to me, "Stop! Look at all those who love you and want to help." So I did. He then said to me that every time I denied someone an opportunity to provide the things I needed, I was denying someone a blessing. Well, that really struck a chord with me, as a good many of us have been raised to believe in pride and self-sufficiency.

I believed that asking or receiving help was a sign of weakness. Well, I couldn't have been at a weaker and more vulnerable point in my life than at that moment. It was the words "denying someone a blessing" that made sense. Aren't we here to serve each other? It's my opinion that the difference between Heaven and Hell is sharing versus selfishness. Was I being passively and unconsciously selfish? Yep, I was, so I now ask anyone willing to offer a helping hand for help openly. I now call people up and accept offers when I need to. Most importantly, I now understand what I need to understand while in the earth plane, so hopefully I'm earning a few brownie points with whatever awaits us on the other side.

Honestly, you can only use so many of your girlfriends' husbands and brothers before they start to hide from you. There does come a time when you're going to have to hire someone for the job that's way too hard to do yourself. So, ask around and find that reliable plumber, electrician, and handyman, because sooner or later you're going to need them. I figure they've got a family to feed, and by paying them you get some of those brownie points from the divine.

When you're paying them, they're going to show up. Fortunately for me, I've been blessed with so many loving people that I really haven't had a problem so serious that I couldn't wait to have it fixed if there were ever to be a no-show. From time to time, a no-show can happen. People have their own lives with their own demands. You're not always their priority, so just breathe and the help will come or you'll figure it out alone.

Chuck wasn't the wealthiest man I had ever been with by any stretch of the imagination, so there wasn't anything to worry about other than typical worries about homelessness and starvation. I manage as best I can and use what skills I have to the best of my ability to satisfy my needs. It works, but by no means is it a materialistic success story.

Here is where I can acknowledge my gratitude for what we do have. I purchased my own home, which I struggle to keep by myself. I've traded my vehicles. I'm grateful for having the strength to be a single woman in what is still a man's world. Where is the fairy tale ending? I've watched way too many little girl chick flicks with Charlie Anne, and it's kind of getting to me. Miss Charlie Anne will often respond to my exasperated thoughts about the unrealistic fairy tales, and she'll say, "I know, I know, Momma. Prince Charming isn't real. Can we watch the movie now?" Poor thing. I'm grateful she loves me.

I came into my marriage with my own tools. That's yet another blessing of being a late-in-life momma. I learned a lot of do-it-yourself stuff long before I knew Chuck. I married him because he was a bad ass in the kitchen-HA!

Feeling vulnerable...

I absolutely felt vulnerable after Chuck died, and I'm still working on vulnerability. As time has gone on, I'm feeling more powerful and less vulnerable. I guess it just comes down to adjusting to my new role as a single momma. With each new experience and with each new triumph, I'm feeling less and less vulnerable. I'm still accumulating good experiences that are helping me feel more powerful. I think it's true when they say not to mess with momma bear and her cubs! This momma bear is learning to be quite self-sufficient and takes good care of her cubs.

CHAPTER NINE

Philosophy
The strength, wisdom, and beliefs that helped us then and are helping us now.

It is not uncommon, when one loses a loved one, for the survivor to come to an interesting awareness. There doesn't seem to be much that separates life from death, and it feels as though the veil between life and death is thin and one can go right through and yank the person back, or we can jump through the veil and join the recently departed. In the shock of the first moments, the brain thinks, "If it is that easy to go then just come back. That must be easy also." It is difficult for the non-traumatized mind, the rational mind, to comprehend this type of thinking process, but it seems possible to the mind that is reeling with a sudden shock. As time goes on, it feels like the person floats further and further away. The veil seems thicker, and the mind eventually realizes the loved one cannot be yanked back. Gone is gone.

TRISH

During those thirty-six intertwined years, we learned about our little quirks, idiosyncrasies and things we like and don't like, but most importantly, we nurtured our love. We laughed together and cried together. We kept each other grounded in times of need. We were each other's best friend, lover, confidant, and rock…and then, BAM! It's all gone in a flash! It felt like I was treading in uncharted waters.

Reality felt harsh, unfair and unkind, but every night while writing, I examined myself as a single woman by looking at possible new opportunities that I could create while always repeating my daily mantra: "That was then and this is now!"

When sadness or anger over a memory would pop up, I would write about it and examine it as a therapist would for her client. I called on my higher self for counseling, and my higher self always showed me another way to choose to look at the past. I call it reframing. I never changed the facts, but I changed the way I perceived the facts. In writer lingo, I changed the "story" by rewriting the old "chapters" as I learned new ways of perceiving them. The sadness and anger would often quickly dissolve, creating an opening toward a healthier, new identity. I could feel I was healing slowly but surely, as healing has been a very gradual process.

As a lifelong student of Taoism, which I view as a philosophy and not a religion, my philosophy on death was fairly well-formed at the time of Bob's transition. I understood, and still do, the non-permanence of life and that change is a part of the natural order of life. I also believe that nothing dies; it just changes into something different, and the cycle continues.

Fortunately, I can view my nearly daily spiritual practice of meditation and prayer as a blessing at the time Bob was in the intensive care unit near the end of his life because when I paid attention to my spiritual practices, they guided me and kept my emotions on a more even keel through the human pain and suffering.

However, there was a brief window of time early on after Bob's passing when I thought I should just yield to my higher self and push away the pain and suffering. Quite frankly, I was growing tired of grieving. In other words, I thought I should know better than to allow myself to cling to the past when experiencing the rushes of intense pain and sorrow that at times would randomly appear out of thin air. Then I arrived at a fork in the road along this journey. I had a choice to make, and the choice I made was to allow the pain and suffering to pass through me by acknowledging it but not clinging to it. I finally came to accept that expressing pain and suffering is just a part of being human, just as there are various ways to express love and compassion.

It was about a year and some after his passing when I came to the realization that Bob left me with a gift of a new understanding about the soul's evolution. With a manuscript about harmony and balance waiting for editing that I had written years ago, accompanied by a visual model of harmony and balance that I had received as a gift from my vast and unlimited creative higher self in the early 1990s, I now had an expanded understanding of how the soul evolves. Simply put, we arrive in this realm to raise our consciousness for our soul's continued evolution by choosing to rise above the fray of any perceived negative appearances to create a life of harmony and balance. We are here to increase our capacity to give and receive love. Thus, our soul evolves. Through the experience of letting go of the attachment to the painful emotions that do not define who I am, my soul is evolving with the grace of time.

I believe everyone who has experienced a loss of a husband or partner finds their own unique path when learning how to live a new life. For me, it was a day-to-day experience, as I am sure it is for most. There is no right or wrong way to learn how to live a new life, and there is no expiration date on the amount of time you need to grieve. Personally, I was stretching myself in ways I had never been stretched. This widowhood experience was brand new to me, and just like motherhood, it didn't come with a manual. However, I made a choice about how I wanted to approach building my new life. A choice, you ask? Allow me to explain.

I live a daily life where I consciously strive for harmony and balance, as I've shared briefly in the introduction, which perhaps requires further explanation for this chapter so I can better explain how I'm learning to build my new life.

In my take on life, we are here in this existence to experience opportunities for our soul to evolve. Simply put, we are here to increase our capacity to share love. Now, the key to the soul's evolution is striving to maintain a life of harmony and balance that will always be found in the present moment...not in the past, nor in the future. This is where my world of grief appeared to collide with living a life in the present moment. I felt my emotions were playing out on a see-saw.

On the one hand, my emotions were undoubtedly rooted in the past. I missed him! I was angry at him for leaving me and our family so early on. I was so disappointed that we didn't fulfill our second half of our life together.

On the other hand, I wasn't sure who I was anymore. Rooted in the past thirty-six intertwined years with Bob was a large part of my identity as his wife, his lover, best friend and business partner that had been cultivated and nurtured. On that fateful day in August when he had departed forever, so had those parts of my identity. The loss of that part of my identity after he passed on caused me to feel unsettled in a way that led to moments of fear, anxiety and at times paralysis when I thought about my uncertain future.

I knew I couldn't move toward a more harmonious and balanced life in that state of mind, so I chose how I was going to begin the process of healing. I didn't give myself a deadline. I'm not that rigid! I just took it a day at a time. I chose to utilize the four principles that I had written in a manuscript several years ago on reestablishing harmony and balance, and they are as follows: intent, love, forgiveness, and gratitude. However, I've added a new exercise that complemented the four principles—creating new memories.

Intent: My intent is two-fold. The first intent, which is to strive to live more in the present moment, played an important role in the success of the second intent—to create a new identity of my own making. They both work hand in hand.

Love: I knew love would be my guiding force, especially through the more difficult parts of the grieving process. I made a choice to express my innate nature wherever I went, to extend an extra dose of love to the people I was with or the nature that surrounded me. Over time, I found myself smiling more often than crying, and I was beginning to create wonderful new experiences that would become pleasant memories over time. I learned the more I opened my heart to extend love, the more love I was capable of receiving. That felt so wonderful. Love is a soothing and gentle healing medicine.

Forgiveness: Forgiveness didn't come that easily at first, but I knew it was absolutely necessary during my healing process. I felt a lot of anger toward Bob for leaving my life. I felt angry at myself for not being able to do more to save his life. I was angry for having to make all the huge changes by myself. I had a mountain of forgiveness to tackle. This part of the process has been ongoing. However, in the past year, the feelings and thoughts needing forgiveness have become very infrequent. When something that needs forgiveness does arise, it is an opportunity to forgive quickly, and if it pops up again, I forgive it again. From experience, I know the day will come when I will have completely forgiven everything.

Gratitude: Gratitude was a daily exercise, and just like forgiveness, it also didn't come that easily at first. However, over time and when I felt ready, I trained myself to find something, anything, related or unrelated, to be grateful for after a sad moment. I would sit with the sad thought and heavy heart. I processed it, made a conscious decision to allow it to pass, and immediately followed it up with a moment of gratitude. Usually, I didn't have to look far to find moments. I was grateful for my family and friends. I was grateful for my home. I was grateful for the time I did have with Bob. I was even grateful for a sunny day. I was grateful for all I had in the present moment and all that was still to come. After a round of feeling the strong and wonderful emotions of gratitude, my heart would always feel better.

Creating new memories: Creating new memories is just as important as the other four principles. You can't create new memories when feeling stuck on or attached to all the old memories. I took this in small steps. A month after Bob passed on would have been his birthday; two months later would be Thanksgiving, and a month after that would be Christmas. Just the mere thought of those important dates coming up sent me into a state of sadness, but I also seized the opportunity to start creating new memories. "Start" was the key word. On the day of the important dates or holidays, I made a conscious decision to stay focused on the present moment, extend my love to everyone I was visiting, and have gratitude for the experience, but it didn't always go as smoothly as one would think based on my description here. There were those brief moments of sadness while driving home alone and walking into an empty house. However, I kept up the work, and with each passing year, my new happy memories are starting to soften the sad feelings about the past.

Was this healing process a walk in the park? No, it wasn't. As my good friend, Connie, pointed out to me early on, I was too hard on myself at times and my impatience was showing. I was grateful for her observation because it showed me that I needed to lighten up on myself. I needed to love myself more. I've come to understand maintaining harmony and balance by using the principles above is a very important part of taking care of the self, especially while healing. Be more gentle, and more gentleness will follow.

The process has been gradual, spanning the past three years, and I can happily report that I am doing very well and I am actually having fun discovering and shaping a new identity. In a way, it is sort of like cleaning out a closet—discarding the old things that no longer serve me while keeping the good things that serve me well.

PEGGY

Early on, I realized that when I tried to make what *was* reality match what I *wanted* reality to be, I experienced pain and sorrow. I wanted Dan to be here, but he wasn't, so I was trying to make the thoughts match and they couldn't. Part of my mind acknowledged he wasn't here, and the other part was trying to make him here. It was painful trying to make those thoughts come together and match up. It is difficult for me to put this concept into words. When I allow myself to become clear with the reality that he is not here, then I can focus on my next step. Realizing the wisdom of not trying to make two opposite thoughts match freed up my energy to focus on what was good in my life, what I was grateful for, and how I could create a new, joy-filled life.

It is important to keep in mind that losing a loved one is a significant event. It is a huge change to adjust to. The pain and tears we feel are real and normal. Our reactions are all part of the human experience. It's not something to feel ashamed about, run away from, or apologize for. Our sorrow and grief is a process, not a destination. Feel them, experience them, take a breath, and take another step in the present moment.

The human truth is, when we live, we die. Life and death are part of the same cycle. When we love, we lose. No matter what we love or whom we love, that love is going to change at some point.

Death of a loved one does not stop us from living or

loving again. Knowing love is going to be lost at some point does not stop us from loving again, and again, and again.

Experiencing a serious loss causes us to "reset." We must reset our perspective on life, on faith, on what it takes to be happy, on what joy is, and on rediscovering "who I am." We are faced with reevaluating what we want in life and how we relate to other people.

We need to hit the reset button and start life again. We reset many of our perspectives because we are no longer doing things to affect two people. We're doing things to affect one person.

I've done a lot of thinking about life because of my experiences as a caregiver. I grew up in a country setting with pets and animals, so I experienced life and death often. I was close to my mother's parents and, as a teenager, experienced their deterioration and deaths. I think some of my philosophy came with me from youth, and some of it came through later years after reading a lot of self-development books. In large part, I have also done a lot of introspection and tapping into the inner wisdom that is available for all of us.

My friend Carol lost her husband years ago to suicide. Recently, we were talking about the grieving process, and she shared some wisdom gained from her experience: "We learn we cannot die with the dead. Instead we live for the living." That's true. After Dan died, I found myself saying to loved ones as I reminded myself, "Dan died. I didn't."

During the first year I developed a simple philosophy about the human condition. "When we live, we die. When we love, we lose." At some point in any and every relationship, life shifts. To resist that reality is to unnecessarily burden ourselves with pain. It is easier said than done, but it does not change the idea that human life and love are mortal. For all the years humans have been living and dying, I would offer that we are not very good at it. Each death seems like the first in human history. Much like each birth seems like the first birth in human history and happy, young parents feel they are the first to experience the great joy and wonder of welcoming a precious offspring into their lives. Both joy and grief come with being human.

I also remember one morning toward the end of the first year or early into the second, as I was getting into the shower, I started saying aloud, "I am not a victim, I am *not* a victim, *I am not* a victim." No one did this to me, no one took my husband from me on purpose. He had an accident, and I was alone. I was alone because I was alive. I was alive, and I had three sons who were missing their father. I had grandkids, siblings, and friends who missed Dan. I had long appreciated being alive and having the opportunity to make a positive difference in the world, but I knew I would be even more grateful and appreciative of every day I was alive. I would be aware of how fleeting life can be. I would be even more aware than I had been that this day could be my last and the words and deeds I speak and do today may be my last. Every day and every word counts.

JENNIFER

I have been blessed with knowing such a culturally diverse group of people over the years. Because of them, I have welcomed many philosophies that I'm still trying to incorporate into my everyday life to help me make sense of all this and to heal. My Christian friends provide me with familiar scriptures from my childhood. I've been given scripture for several Eastern philosophies that have really resonated with my soul, providing me hope and comfort.

I also feel if you are outside in nature, Mother Earth herself will help you to heal. There is something to be said about observing the natural world we all seem so disconnected from today. I highly recommend that you go outside whenever you can and watch the clouds drift by for a while. If you have children, take them with you and listen to the sounds of the world that surrounds you. That means listening to the wind rustling through the leaves on the trees, the cicadas, the crickets, the birds…well, you get the idea. It will slow that monkey brain down for a moment, or let him loose again depending on your needs and abilities to create stillness. I'm not always good at stillness, but I am practicing and trying to teach my young ones. However, I am good at letting the monkey thoughts form and learning to allow them to pass on by, just like the clouds.

I take one moment at a time. Get that? ONE moment at a time. A moment according to Ayurveda is the amount of time it would take one to breathe in deeply and slowly through inhalation and exhalation three times. That's how I've made it this far. I still find myself starting to panic and get overwhelmed at times, so I stop for a moment and just breathe. Does that work as often as I'd like? No, but when it does, it's amazing. Are you starting to see an overall pattern reflected in my answers to the questions so far? It's all about time. Moving through grief takes time, just as it takes time to move through life. You can only go as fast as you are able or as slow as you need. Breathe!

With much relief as I look back, the greatest choice I

made was to surrender. I'm certain that this was the second time in the entirety of my life that I was able to do so by letting go of any and all expectations and just observing the flow of love from the people that came into our lives during the time of Chuck's departure. If you want to believe in miracles, grieving a loved one is a good time to watch them happen. I think we all get so caught up in trying to take control of all the huge changes that occur after our loved one leaves. We don't truly understand that we aren't in control of one dang thing because our grieving emotions are attached to our ego, and our ego has a need to feel in control. We should be learning to align our emotions with the pure love in our heart. It is in our heart where our real power and guidance lies. We will receive miracles when we surrender to the pure love within the divine.

I had called out fairly consistently to Chuck on a nightly basis for several years until one day, when I was sitting in a lecture with Dr. Lad at the Ayurvedic Institute, something struck me. The thought had probably been building up over the length of time I had spent reading the great spiritual writings of many religions and great sages, but the thought hadn't been fully realized until that one moment when Dr. Lad said in so many words, "As long as you keep calling him to you, he will never progress on his own path." It's been fairly recent that I've embraced the idea of allowing him to be dead in this physical plane and allowing him to move forward onto the path of his own soul's journey without me. Yes, knowing, or coming to understand, that this earthly journey can be a really lonely one sucks. We may have loved ones all around us all the time, but truly it's a singular experience of growth here.

Learning to live a new life is one of those lessons I already have experience with from when I was younger, and I'm still working on it in this new phase of my life without Chuck. It's really a process of learning to adjust to life and its new set of circumstances. I thought of this saying just now: "Life is what happens while you make plans." Now isn't that the truth? We all have plans for our future when we are with our loved one, but then that day comes when he leaves the physical plane. Bam! Just like that, the plans change. Breathe.

It's a little more difficult for me to make long-term plans and goals because I have the young ones. The near future isn't such a big deal, even though it's fairly new for me, now that both kids are in school. This is also where I'd like to apply the laws of synchronicity. Quite possibly our loved ones, ancestors, or God are showing us the way to a good future if we leave ourselves open to all possibilities. The trick—and I'm still learning to be more consistent in this area—is to leave myself open to the forces beyond my understanding and trust that I'm being guided into areas of life that will create the greatest change for me and my family. It comes and goes for me right now, but I definitely remember a time when I went along with everything that appeared as the "right opportunity" because it felt good and it felt right. There were those time when two people from separate groups would say the exact same words or give me the exact same sign that I needed in that moment. I really want to believe in the magic of this, so I practice this as often as I can. One moment at a time baby, and breathe!

CHAPTER TEN

―――――ＷＷ――――――

Creating My Own Space
Making a conscious decision to move from
"our space" to "my space"

TRISH

It was more painful for me to see his clothing hanging in the closet, his toiletries in a shared bathroom drawer or his coats hanging in the hall closet than it was for me to bag up those items within the first month of his passing. I was very sad at first when I prepared to give away his coats, but strangely enough, I immediately realized how much roomier my coat closet had become.

"I would gladly give up this roomier closet if you could come back," I thought. I kept his two favorite sweatshirts that are enormous on me because I love to snuggle in them during the cold winter months. I've also kept his collection of Hawaiian shirts, many of which were purchased in Hawaii. Recently, I gave two of them away to Harvey, our good friend that stood by Bob's side and the family's during his stay in the ICU.

When the kids asked me what I wanted for Christmas, I requested from my daughter, Räna, that I wanted her to redecorate my living room and for my son, Justin, to move the TV/stereo equipment into the family room. For thirty-six years, I had compromised the design of the living room based on what made Bob comfortable and my taste in decorating. He liked having the TV and stereo equipment in the living room and a loveseat recliner to rest on and to share with me when listening to music or our favorite TV shows, but every time I walked in the front door, all I could painfully see was Bob reclining in the loveseat and another abrupt reminder he wasn't ever going to be sitting there again. However, the project exceeded my expectations!

The kids did a great job. The living room now reflects my personality with peaceful accents of nature throughout. The family room is now suitable for comfortable TV watching or listening to music along with informal entertaining. Having the fireplace in that room made it a warm and cozy place to write for the next three winters following Bob's passing. Why not write in the office? I couldn't write in the office because it became the most difficult room to transform into my own. The office is where Bob and I worked together on several manuscripts, class agendas, and public speaking notes. The office is where Bob kept all of his awards, certificates, and any personal mementos filed in various desk drawers. Basically, I abandoned the office altogether for the first year and a half.

With each passing day, the office became a reminder for me to deal with the memories tied to the room. I grew tired of not dealing with it, so I tackled it over a two-week period. I knew there wasn't a rush, but the longer I didn't deal with it, the longer it would take for the healing to occur. Slowly but surely, I packed up his mementos and placed them in pretty plastic boxes to store them with the thought that I would make sure the kids would be the recipients of their dad's life story one day. I did find a well-written children's story he'd written and some wonderful poetry, all writings he had never shared with me nor did I have an inkling they even existed 'til then...so sad.

Here I am in the present day in a rearranged room with freshly painted walls, new window shades and a new framed graphic picture Räna made and gave to me for Christmas two years ago that thoughtfully quotes the Pink Floyd song called "Breathe." It says:

"Long you live and high you fly
and smiles you give and tears you'll cry
and all you touch and all you see
is all your life will ever be."

I moved the comfy loveseat from the living room into the office. I've moved back in, gradually, and now it's my office. It feels good.

I decided to keep the pickup truck. With the nonprofit, it has come in handy. Besides, I enjoy driving it, and it's my grandson Kade's favorite mode of transportation when we get together!

PEGGY

Two or three years after Dan left, I had the thought, "Oh! I can put this here. I can move that there. If it works for me, I can do it. This is *my* space." I remember having that conscious thought. This is *my* house. It was hard to get used to saying "my" house instead of "our" house. For forty-two years I was part of "we," "us," and "our." That is a hard shift to make.

While he was alive, my routine was to take Dan's shirts to the cleaners while he was out of town working during the week. He would then have fresh shirts to wear when he came home. For several days after Dan died, I kept saying, "I've got to take Dan's shirts to the cleaners." Finally, my sister Rita asked, "Why? He's not going to wear them again." That was a dose of reality I had been missing. Back into the cleaner's bag those shirts went. Almost five years later, they're still in the bag. On occasion, I have pulled them out, put them on, and hugged myself. Sometimes I hug them and drink in the fragrance of his scent. This happened more in the first three years than it does presently.

About two months after Dan died, I sold his truck. I wanted to keep it, but my car was more practical for me and I only wanted one car to drive, maintain, and insure. Selling his truck was an emotional experience. Luckily, my brother and his wife stood by me as I sold it. Ugh! I'll forever be grateful for their support.

Moving Dan's material goods to new homes has been a gradual process. I would like to really turn the page, lighten my load, and simplify my life in general. Much of Dan's clothing was taken to Goodwill and other charities in the first weeks. Finding new homes for Dan's material goods is an ongoing process. I'm still dealing with some clothing and tools.

One of my methods of reducing the goods is to load up a box, drive to Goodwill, unload, and drive away without looking back. Early on, I would cry as I drove away. Now, that rarely happens. I just drive away and hope that the clothing or tools will bless someone who is alive and well, who can make use of what Dan no longer needs.

There were many days I felt utterly overwhelmed by the amount of work that lay before me. At about the three-year mark I made peace with walking past all the piles, stacks, and boxes that tauntingly resided in my garage. During this time I thought, "I'll address this project when I can. Until then I still love myself." At five years, I have taken care of much of the job, but I still have much more to go before completion.

JENNIFER

I didn't have the opportunity to stay in the space Chuck and I lived in. Truth be told, the man we were financing from "politely" threw us out. He was not a nice guy, let me tell you. There's no doubt he lost some karma brownie points on that one. See, when your spouse dies, and you didn't think about credit scores or building large amounts of credit, you wake up to the harsh rules. I don't like debt, so I've never created any significant debt. Guess what came to my surprise? Someone with bad debt is more eligible for borrowing more money than someone that's got minimal debt. Whatever! So, we moved shortly after Miss Charlie Anne was born. I knew Chuck was a bit of a hoarder, but oh my! Really, Chuck? The first two places we lived in, you would've thought I was a lying and cheating wife because all his stuff dominated our space. As time passed, all his precious stereo equipment stopped working for one reason or another. I miss the movie theater sound and the powerful clarity behind the music. Nothing lasts forever, and that's for sure.

Clearing Chuck's personal belongings has been an

ongoing and gradual process. Looking back, it seems to me that the first and easiest thing to purge is the clothing. When that closet is empty, be ready for a dose of aftershock. Lord, I knew someone else could use the clothes, but that empty space can really be shocking in an unexpected way. I've even emptied out a few closets. Y'all know by now, Chuck was a hoarder of sorts, so I suspect I'll be hauling something of his out of the house for the rest of my life. The thing is, when it's your partner's stuff, the vibration of the experience goes straight to the bone. I'm still surrounded by so many of his things. Here's another confession: I still have so much of his stuff that I'm slowly letting go of. I don't want to be weighed down with attachments any longer. I'll always have the memories, but I just don't need the "stuff."

I'm feeling grateful for having established my, let's just call it, unique sense of self. When the kids and I were able to buy the house we are in now, I decided to let go of more of the silly attachments that were so much a part of my life with Chuck. I'm still on this living journey and he's not. There are moments since Chuck has been gone when our past together feels so distant, and I often find myself questioning my own memories as I go through his belongings each time. I've learned these personal items are so irrelevant and it really is our memories that are most important, whether they are complete truth or not.

CHAPTER ELEVEN

——————————— WW ———————————

Sex and the Reluctant Single Woman
Shifting perspective from married to single

TRISH

Do I consider myself a single woman?...

I consider myself a single person now, but in the beginning, while I was holding tightly to the raw emotions of grieving, I still felt married. I feel this is only normal. Gradually, as I embraced my new identity, I can say I no longer feel married.

Learning to live as a single person has been a gradual process. I now initiate gatherings with my friends and happily accept invitations from others. I haven't totally adjusted to not having companionship at home. I am an extrovert, and I enjoy sharing my life with others. My two kitties just don't quite fill that void, but I do have good friends and family that do their best to fill in the gaps.

I'll always love Bob. He will forever have a special place

reserved in my heart. After all, we raised two beautiful children together. However, I feel you can have more than one great love in a lifetime. I feel this way because love is as unique as the human appearance. Love is limitless and infinite, and there will always be room in my heart for another love. Each relationship is going to be different from the only one I've known for the past thirty-nine years, and I know some parts of new relationships may feel similar to my relationship with Bob, but this is a part of the wonderful and fulfilling human experience!

Am I ready for dating?...

I am looking forward to dating and having another meaningful relationship one day when the opportunity presents itself. I am in no hurry because I am still exploring my new identity, but if the right man comes along, such as another soul mate, I wouldn't hesitate to engage in a new relationship. I miss interacting with male energy. I would like to have a meaningful second half of life and for whoever I meet next to be compatible with me on many levels. The most important part of developing a relationship is to have fun without a lot of drama. I'm a realist. I know drama will always play a part in any relationship, especially if one gets sick, or there is an abrupt change in one's life, such as a death in the family or that of a close friend. I'm very well prepared for such an experience. What I don't want is an excessive amount of negative friction between myself and my new partner. I'd like to be with someone who understands the importance of family, including grandchildren, as I do. I'd like to be with someone who is content staying home, and yet enjoys traveling and exploring. I'm a romantic at heart, and I look forward to giving and receiving little sentiments. I want the opportunity to have a mature relationship from the start, and I have a strong feeling it's not far off. How do I know this? By letting go of the emotional ties to the past, I'm allowing myself to be open and receptive to new possibilities and opportunities!

Do I wear my wedding ring?...

Actually, I still wear it on rare occasions if my wardrobe warrants it! Not that it is a symbol of still being married; I just happen to be very fond of my non-traditional wedding ring that was designed only eleven years before he passed on. Would I stop wearing it entirely if "Mr. Right" came along? Yes, as long as he can replace it with something I would love even more-HA!

While my sister Allison was visiting around my birthday in March, we happened to peek into a classy jewelry store and a certain ring caught my attention. The dynamics behind the reason I was going to wait until another man would replace my wedding ring with something I love even more changed. It just so happens that my "special someone" is my wonderful sister.

Trying a dating website...

During a conversation with the other two Wonder

Widows, the question was asked if we would ever try a dating website and I emphatically said, "No! I have no intention of ever doing so. I've heard horror stories from friends."

Being "hit on" by men...

So far, I can't recall a moment where I was being "hit" on, but then again, maybe I didn't really notice. I've been fairly busy building my writing career and running my nonprofit. Plus, I've enjoyed my friendships with many friends, so I've only been in the position of returning a few smiles but nothing more.

PEGGY

Do I consider myself a single woman?...

It's a funny thing, because after being attached for so long, married when I was eighteen and married for forty-two years, we grew together like two trees growing into one. Our connection caused us to consider the other in every decision and choice we made. Whether we were together physically or not, he was with me, emotionally and spiritually. He was always in my heart. What makes that stop? Nothing! It continues even when the physical form is gone. For practical matters, I know I am single and must take care of myself, but the heart is still in love with Dan.

If a new partnership became a reality, I would not feel

guilty in the least. I am pragmatic enough to be able to add a new love to my tapestry. No, I do not expect a new love interest to take the place of Dan, nor would I compare him to Dan. It is possible he could be quite different. That's okay. I hope to assess Mr. New Man on his own merits.

Affection doesn't just go away. Love doesn't end at the grave…or cremation urn. Having a loving sex partner is certainly something I miss, but I believe I can make a happy life without that part. My hormones are not driving me to quickly pair up just to have sex. I am content enough.

Am I ready for dating?...

Good question. I *think* I am. I really like and appreciate men. I loved being a partner. I miss being a partner. Having a companion sounds like a good idea.

This is a tricky question. I am ready to have new friendships and ease into a more serious relationship but I am not desperate to take on someone else's complications. My life is interesting and pleasant and I do not feel incomplete. I can financially support myself and I have wonderful grown children and friends I like to spend time with.

I had a very good partnership with Dan. Over the years we experienced joys and sorrows, easy times and hard times, ups and downs and at the end of his life, and the end of our partnership, we were best of friends, satisfied lovers, and great travel buddies looking forward to retirement fun. I am grateful for the experience I had with Dan.

Dating? In my heart, I feel I am ready to have a fresh

start with a new man and create a whole new life. That means dating, doesn't it?

In a nutshell, I'd really enjoy a comfortable meeting and dating experience, but I am not going to force the issue. I believe I can continue to create a good life on my own, if that is what happens.

Do I wear my wedding ring?...

To wear the wedding ring or not is a question widows face. I wore my wedding ring for months after Dan died. For a time, I wore it on a necklace. Then I put it in a drawer. I wear it from time to time as the mood strikes me.

Trying a dating website...

From time to time, friends suggest I use a dating website to meet men. No, I am not comfortable with the idea of dating a stranger. Some friends have had experiences that were less than wonderful. Actually, they were downright scary. Nope. No online dating for me.

Being "hit on" by men...

I'm not entirely comfortable being with other men. It seems they are ready to get friendlier than I am. There have been three opportunities to attend dance events. I've been sensitive about being held too tightly on the dance floor. I just wanted to dance. I wasn't looking for a new life partner or a regular dance partner. I have my limits, and there have been some awkward moments.

JENNIFER

Do I consider myself a single woman?...

I'd say I'm pretty darn single. What sums it up is that I'm paying the bills and raising my children independently of a man. My "insane" conversations on the front porch are mine and mine alone. I do miss having someone eating dinner with us. For that matter, it would be nice to have someone take us out to dinner once in a while. Oh, the single life as a middle-aged mother of small children! Young and single widow ladies, let me share with you this part of my journey.

Oh my goodness when Chuck was dying, so was my sex life. There it all was, just dying with him. I love sex. I wish women had more courage to embrace their sexuality without fear or guilt.

I'm not even showing signs of menopause! I'm a full functioning woman with a desire for sex. I'm a little worrisome at the idea of pregnancy, but surely God's sense of humor won't go there with me, and yes, I believe in protection!

Hormones at my age are fun stuff all right, because when you stop nursing, the hormones come flooding back, trying to get you back on the wagon. That was my true introduction into "Self Care"! So, I hauled my little butt down to the self-serve store to learn about this forbidden art. Insert the Hallelujah song here! I had no idea just how much stress, tension, and anxiety can melt away in about five minutes. Ladies, a vibrator is intense! I highly recommend one. It saved my life. Now don't get me wrong, it's a great thing, but a real man? There's no comparison! I hear how liberating it is to go through menopause and be free of mood swings and desires, so I sit here wondering just what all I'll experience when I enter the "wise woman" phase. Any feedback on this liberating experience is always welcome so long as it's of a nurturing nature. So, ladies, have fun with toys and find some pleasure in your singularity. And for heaven's sake, love your female body. Truly, it's a gift to be treasured.

Am I ready for dating?...

From what I've seen, men by now are at an age where they have almost grown children or do have grown children and are looking for a traveling companion. Some men are having a crazy midlife crisis and think a really young woman will help them to relive their youth. Of course, there are a great many scenarios between, but those two are pretty much what I have encountered so far. Sometimes I feel like it wouldn't be so bad to find a long-lost crush either.

After Chuck died I didn't have the capacity to see that far into the future, but it wasn't until I decided I had to let Chuck be dead that I started to warm up to the idea of letting someone new come into my life—well, someone brave enough for all that's me. Now, when I say I had to let Chuck be dead, what I meant was, I needed to quit holding his spirit hostage to this physical plane to satisfy my inability to let go of our connection. Have I been completely successful with that? Heck no! I do, however, ask Chuck if he can come and comfort me a little more often. Sometimes I don't care and just demand comfort from him, like I have control— HA! I realize there's no possible way anyone here on earth could ever possibly know the details of what goes on in the nonphysical plane.

There were way too many absent years. And yes ladies, the six years of being dry and not having sex with a living, breathing person has finally come to an end. Vibrators and whatnot should be discussed way more among women seeing how well it helped me during the dry spell. I was needlessly wondering how someone would want to be with a woman chasing ghosts. I still don't know if I hold onto Chuck any more than anyone else grieving a loved one, but I do seem to have a better level of acceptance of where I am in this life, though not as glamorous as a day dreamer might have imagined. Sex can be so fabulous, and I have to confess how wonderful it felt just to feel that masculine presence again next to my body. Oh my goodness, to feel desired and desirable was, and is, amazing.

For those of you that live with a Tiny Tyrant or two and are trying to pick up a few tips on how to handle sex when there are kids around, I recently discovered a book that the title alone will forever be imprinted in my head: "Nobody Likes a Cockblock" by R. Swanson. Now, I've not had the chance to full-on read this adult book written in children's style about woodland creature moms and dads just trying to get their swerve on, but when you've had years alone with your children, they don't truly understand they can't just barge into the bedroom anymore. It seems like an appropriate book for my situation. I'm just grateful I had everyone in their own beds before all this new "lovin'" began.

I'm good with "your place or mine" for right now. The idea of growing old with someone is kind of shattered a bit in my story, so I say, just enjoy a good love story and hold on tightly in case it should go tragically downhill. Let me explain. I found out in my new relationship that some old thoughts and feelings left over from my previous relationship with Chuck can trigger my grief response, and the triggered grief has been unbelievably harsh for my new man as well.

The triggers will no doubt mess with you, but hopefully your experience has given you a strength and wisdom that won't create such an intense feeling as mine. I have come to understand I have posttraumatic stress syndrome (PTSD). Yeah! I don't even know what to say about all of that. I just know that trying to process even a bit of the grief often leads to a fear of sudden loss and death. If you can relate to my experience, don't be ashamed of having those feelings and find a good counselor. I highly recommended it. My only regret is I didn't start counseling earlier.

Do I wear my wedding ring?...

I took my wedding ring off when I was pregnant with Charlie Anne because it was a little tight from the fluids and whatnot. I ended up taking Chuck's off a few weeks later, when he began his first journey into the hospital. I never put it back on. Live in the moment.

Trying a dating website...

Oh God, yes. I never mentioned I was a widow unless specifically asked about my past relationships. It's surprising how much another will talk about themselves before even considering your experience. I've heard a few of their stories, and some men were way too cut and dried about what they wanted in a relationship or even in a hookup. What I've experienced, and I'm not looking for a hookup, is that some men may have very well had way too many partners for me to feel physically safe. It's a crazy thing, this online dating. As with all forms of communication that's not in-person, be prepared for downright ignorant rudeness. I'm confident in my body and skin, so typically, I got out okay. If you're a widow, I wish you good luck with dating sites.

Being "hit on" by men...

Sleep deprivation and nursing a baby doesn't attract too many good men. I think I would have been a little concerned by someone hitting on me with a baby. Yes, I was, and always will be, with my children until they are grown.

I have always been sensitive to men hitting on me. Many get horribly aggressive when rejected, and if you try to be polite, they think you're flirting or playing with them. Unfortunately, trying to be polite is a misguided behavior taught to girls. Sometimes we should be fearless with our decisions. Hell knows what goes on in the brains of some men. Yes, I'm afraid of a certain type of man. Thank you for those of you men that understand what I'm saying. I guess the benefit of getting older is that I don't get the aggressive behaviors as often any more, perhaps due to my dissipating youthfulness. Here's to the wise women—may we all stand with our younger women to help them change the world.

CHAPTER TWELVE

Self-Care
Hey girlfriend, ain't no one else gonna do it!

TRISH

I can't say enough about how important it is to give yourself care, even though at times you really could care less about self-care after losing a loved one. In the beginning, I found myself not caring if I ate or what I ate if I did. Cooking for myself seemed like a senseless chore. I didn't care if I went without makeup. After all, who was I putting it on for? I did keep up with my hygiene. As a little more time passed, and I began to go out more, I started taking better care of myself. Grief can take such a toll on the physical body, so I started getting deep massages to release any stored stress and started seeing a chiropractor to realign my body. From there, I've been working on realigning my GI tract and clearing my adrenals as well with the help of my chiropractor's expertise in sound nutritional practices. I care about what I ingest in my body, and I am grateful to have access to more organic whole foods. I stock up on nutritional go-to foods since my cooking routine hasn't returned. My diet is not perfect yet, but I know I'm on a good path.

I find a very important part of self-care is to keep experiences lighter through humor. Staying as present as I could allowed me to be open and receptive to humor. My humorous friends, especially Kathy, knew naturally how to make me laugh. In their presence, I nearly always felt the lightest in contrast to the heaviness of my heart. I actually felt more "normal" when I laughed. I found myself watching more comedies than ever before and not because I was avoiding the heartache, but because it felt good!

It is true; laughter is good medicine, especially for a broken heart. Laughter is the antidote to all the pain one feels during the times of grief, even for a brief moment.

"Our body needs laughter as much as it needs tears.
Both are cleansers of stress."
Mahogany Silver-Rain

Giving yourself permission to rest...

For three months I was in perpetual motion, always rushing Bob from one doctor appointment to the next or to a lab to draw blood again first thing in the morning. Or perhaps it was all the discussions with the health insurance company and the logistical planning required to get Bob to the Mayo clinic in Scottsdale, Arizona, that kept me going. Then there were all the countless hours going back and forth between hospitals. Let's include the countless hours spent researching Bob's symptoms or playing nurse when he was back at home…and then on August 21 at 3:05 pm, it all came to an abrupt halt!

I took his sister Ann to the airport on the twenty-second and my sister to the airport one day later and went straight to the funeral home to make arrangements for his body. By the early afternoon, I collapsed on the loveseat and watched *Create TV* on PBS. I would awaken only for brief moments and catch glimpses of various topics from someone teaching how to prepare mushroom soup on top of a mountain in Norway, to a travel log through some European country, but I slept past sunset. I was exhausted beyond description. That is what I call a survival rest, and then there is the healing rest that I didn't have too much understanding about in the beginning, but thankfully, my friends did.

My good friends, Connie, Danelle, and Kathy, gave me "permission" to rest and reminded me to take the necessary time to grieve. This was a steep learning curve for me, for patience wasn't an exemplary virtue of mine. At times I was so tired of being in the depths of grieving that I would ask God to remove the grieving by saying, "Get this off of me now!" as one would gesture getting an army of ants off one's arms! Other times I didn't want to be alone with my feelings and thoughts. This was a signal that I needed to call a friend or my sister. I found that just talking to people, not in desperation, but to have casual, everyday conversations, would cause a shift in my emotions. I am a lifelong practitioner of meditation and a Reiki Master teacher. These two practices helped me tremendously with the grieving process, thankfully so. It wasn't too long before I started getting back on track with everyday life, and duly noted, it has been a very gradual process.

PEGGY

The concept of self-care is very important. I put conscious effort into participating in or being a spectator during happy activities. I watch comedies and listen to music, both recorded and live. I look for events where there is laughter or light-heartedness. These events are highly important to me. Part of what I did to stay connected to comedy, especially in the early years, was to watch comedy skits or interviews on YouTube before bedtime. That helped me go to sleep with a smile on my face.

A few months into the process of learning to reconstruct my life, when sadness was especially heavy, I purchased a ukulele for my granddaughter. One day it occurred to me to purchase a ukulele for myself and learn to play it. I appreciate music very much, but I am not naturally talented. I felt there was wisdom in making myself focus on a new skill that would keep my mind occupied in a positive direction. I never got very good at playing it, but it sure helped me focus on something happy rather than allow sadness to take up permanent residence in my heart and mind.

Within six months of Dan's death, I decided it would be wise to pay a visit to my general medical practitioner, chiropractor, eye doctor, and dentist. I explained that I was recently widowed and just wanted to make sure I was physically healthy. We were in a new part of town, and I was establishing relationships with new practitioners.

My general practitioner mentioned that a psychologist had just joined the group and thought I might want to schedule a visit with her. I did. As I sat down with her in her office,

I said, "I am recently widowed and I just want to make sure I am thinking clearly and I'm not crazy." It turns out, I did her more good than she did me. She had her own troubles, and I shared info that was helpful to her. "Guess I'm not too crazy after all."

Self-care comes in many forms. It can mean drinking more water or better quality water. It can mean eating more or less depending on needs and habits and perhaps eating better, healthier food. It can mean getting more sleep or less, again, depending on needs and habits. Self-care can mean getting exercise, being positively entertained, or participating in an enjoyable activity. Healthy relationships with friends and family are important. Learning to play ukulele was helpful for me. Taking up Zentangle (zentangle.com) and learning to draw for peaceful pleasure was helpful. Zentangle is a good evening activity to help wind down and prepare for sleep without the aid of electronic devices.

Adding high quality supplements to my nutrition regimen has been helpful. Using essential oils for emotional support has been very helpful. Taking aroma-filled baths was helpful. Having open and honest conversations with my friends about my process was helpful. Watching comedy was helpful. Watching beautiful sunrises and sunsets has been helpful. Bringing beautiful flowers into my space has been helpful. Spending time in nature is great for helping me feel grounded and peaceful. Paying attention to my business, which is a business that helps enhance others' lives, is helpful (www.peggyoils.com). The list of ways we can be good to ourselves is long. Different people will find different methods of self-care. The methods we adopt will most likely change over time, and shifts will happen in our process.

In the first months and years especially, I felt very vulnerable and I had no desire to be exposed or on display. I had installed nifty top-down, bottom-up window blinds on the big picture windows that faced the street in the front of my house. Most days the blinds were lowered from the top just enough for me to see the beautiful mountain view through the top portion of the windows and to block others' view into my house. I was comfortable being able to see out but did not want others to see in.

Interestingly, at the time Dan died, the business I am in required me to host large events and present information on stage. I got back in the swing of it several weeks into widowhood. I am quite comfortable on stage, and I doubt anyone could guess how I was feeling inside. At the end of the event I'd pack up, head home, walk into my closet, and sob my eyes out for as long as I needed to.

My business also includes being in contact with many people. Previously, I was very comfortable with this, but I discovered I was now very sensitive to being around a large number of people and a lot of commotion for very long. I found it necessary to pace myself and isolate myself from time to time. I believe this had to do with nervous system overload.

At the beginning of year three, I returned to Costa Rica, where I had been a foreign exchange student in high school. I reunited with my Tican family—my wonderful sister Ligia and my mother Adilia, recently widowed when my father Carlos passed away months before. Their love and compassion was nurturing. It was interesting to find myself in a position to be helpful to Mami Adilia as she journeyed through her first year of life without Papi. I noticed Mami was experiencing some of the same reactions I had in my early years.

As year two began and again in the beginning of year four, I flew to Hawaii to visit in-laws Maureen and Carl. Both Hawaii trips were a combo of business and pleasure. The business, friendships, and ocean fed my soul.

Year five has just begun, and I am preparing for a huge adventure on another continent as part of my self-care. There seems to be a pattern here. I recognize that I enjoy stretches of time at home for months and then get a feeling that I must change my environment. I travel, visit wonderful people in environments far removed from mine, and then I return home to enjoy being in my own home alone for a while until I get the feeling again. I playfully call this feeling "running away." It has been helpful to take lengthy trips at a particular time of year, usually late winter and early spring. This is the time of our wedding anniversary, Dan's death date, and my birthday. It helps to be happily occupied and distracted at those times of year.

Giving yourself permission to rest...

Taking time off and making time to rest is important. That is easier said than done but well worth the effort. Grieving and readjusting takes more energy than one might guess. In this fast-paced world we are a part of, it is easy to feel lazy or guilty for taking time to rest. Especially in the beginning, we must give ourselves permission to nurture ourselves.

Getting into bed by myself is not very satisfactory; there's nobody to talk to and nobody to cuddle with. Reading a book for a bit before dropping off to sleep can be helpful if the book is about a pleasant subject or story.

Gloriann, a very dear woman who married my father

three years after my mother died, helped me understand that grieving takes a lot more energy than we realize. Our culture seems to value busyness, and goodness knows my to-do list was long and never-ending after Dan died. I had to give myself permission to step back from the idea that I had to go, go, go and that I had to accomplish what I thought others wanted me to accomplish on their timeline. It was important to take time to stay connected to family, especially sons, grandchildren, and siblings. This is still not easy to do. I remind myself that I am important and I am the person who is in charge of taking care of myself. Getting adequate rest can be a challenge, but I work at it. I noticed, especially in the early years, when I did get enough rest I was more patient. I was more able to handle tasks. I was more able to handle people. And when I didn't get enough rest, I felt a bit unraveled and impatient.

JENNIFER

When Charlie Anne started Kindergarten, I thought of all the things I could do now. Truth be told, I found myself grieving uninterrupted for the first time since Chuck died, alone. Trust me on this one, I did grieve a tremendous amount the years before with Hayden while nurturing Charlie Anne through infancy. Let me tell you, I found myself so physically exhausted, I don't think I did much but take pajama naps while they were at school. This is what I call self-care personified! Well, the year is up, and I'm still not rested enough or fully up to speed, but I'm hoping this summer will provide amazing opportunities for self-care that I'll recognize. You know, there is a divine message in synchronicity.

CHAPTER THIRTEEN

Creating a New Identity
Discovering a new me

TRISH

Because the threads of my spiritual practice are woven so tightly within me, there was never any doubt that I would one day thrive again. I trusted my inner guidance to show me the way, and sometimes I leaned on my friends when it seemed as though the emotional grieving was blocking my connection to my inner guidance. All in all, I choose to thrive and I choose to learn how to do so, as I am still doing today, during this ongoing process of gradual development. After all, I was very aware that I was, and still am, living in this physical plane. Therefore I'm very motivated to make the best of my experiences here. Also, I know Bob would want me to live a full life consisting of love, peace, prosperity, good health, and happiness. I know Bob would want my soul to have a positive and fulfilling evolution while I am still here.

I'd like to share a journal passage I wrote on June 25, 2016, that may shine more light on the subject of thriving.

The passage was written after Bob's "visit" with me on June 18 and shortly after I was notified that an important meeting for my nonprofit was going to take place soon that I had been waiting for four years.

Just this morning I gave thanks to the guidance from within and then I realized I needed to thank myself for being open and receptive-LOL! That's the real bottom line—one needs to be open and receptive to receiving the guidance. It's really just allowing yourself to be in a natural state in accordance with your "true" self. And what creates and sustains this? Love! Plain and simple. The more experiences I have, the better I can understand and make love a part of my daily life. Therefore, I am grateful for experiences, and I am open and receptive to more experiences.

What I've come to also realize is the importance of learning new things because learning is aiding in the evolution of my soul. And since I live in this physical plane, it is important I apply what I've learned and experienced to my evolution in order to fulfill my soul's purpose here, and that is to aid in the evolution of humankind. I've known my purpose since I was a very young child. My personal evolution and humankind's evolution are working in tandem as mirror images of one another.

The further understanding of my purpose has just entered a higher level of awareness. In order for me to fulfill my higher purpose of aiding the evolution of mankind, I must first apply my purpose to myself by focusing on my own evolution.

I began to think this morning just how fast I'm growing into my higher self. I gave all I could to this growth over the many years I spent nurturing my family. I devoted myself to their well-being while simultaneously putting myself in the background. I separated my role as a mother, wife, and caretaker from my spiritual role of strengthening my connection to my higher self. It felt like there were two "me's" and I lived in two worlds. Those two worlds are blending as one...finally! I have only myself to look after and the time to reacquaint myself with that inner being, my higher self. I'm really having fun tapping into the unlimited riches self-discovery beholds. It's like I was a diamond under pressure for so many years, and now the diamond has surfaced and I'm polishing it and admiring its beauty and potential to shine. I know this is the way my life is meant to be!

I keep seeing Bob's message, the single white butterfly, fluttering about around the deck. I hear him saying, "Fly, baby! Fly!"

Accepting his death...

I began to accept Bob's imminent death while he was in the ICU even though I held out for that miracle right up to, and for a short amount of time beyond, those last few moments, but I was always aware of the reality. The emotions that I was tethered to took quite a bit longer to put in perspective because emotions are what we hold on to when we don't know where our life is going to take us next or we feel there is some greater value in holding on to them. When we don't know what tomorrow or our future life is going to look like, we tend to hold on to what we do know—the past, a past that, for me, included a husband and years of memories.

If I allowed myself to be ruled only by the emotional grieving over Bob leaving me, how could I go on living a life of peace, joy, and happiness? How could I be open and receptive to my inner guidance if my dominant focus was controlled by past emotions?

At times, especially in the beginning, when I allowed the overwhelming emotions of grief to dominate me, I learned to take a breath and realize the experience was providing me with an opportunity to find a balance with my emotions. I didn't succeed the first time, or the second, the third, or the fourth...I think you can get the picture, but over time, I began to see that I had a choice—simmer in emotional turmoil or work on balancing my emotions. I wanted to feel better. I wanted to feel peace, joy, and happiness once again. And then came the time when the balance shifted to wanting to experience the happier feelings more often than wanting to hold on to the past. I began utilizing the technique of acknowledging the emotions (my emotions are okay because they are a part of being human), which allowed them to pass as I envisioned a future of more happiness and joy.

Sometimes I reached out to others so I could process the emotions and work on ways to put them in perspective. It does get easier once you are ready to take action to create a new mindset. A new mindset will create a life of peace, joy, and happiness. Keep in mind, you are not the same person you were when you first got married, and you are not the same person a year, a month, a week, or even a day ago. We are meant to thrive! We are meant to live a life of peace, happiness, and joy! Remember, you can't drive forward while looking through the rearview mirror.

PEGGY

Oh goodness, this is an ongoing process. There are statements I repeat from time to time to remind myself things have changed. In the first two years, it was important to remind myself that Dan is the one who died. I'm still here, I'm still alive, and it is up to me to create a happy life worth living. It really takes some time for new ideas to settle in. I remember that Dan was a really good chapter in my life, and for all the years he was in my life, he was the main attraction, he was the star of my show. He was all-important to me. Now, I must love myself. I'm important, and it's important to take care of myself.

It really was hard to get used to being alone and not being in a partnership. It was very odd, especially for the first three or more years, to make decisions based solely on what I wanted. It is not good or bad, just different and something to adjust to.

Over time I could feel shifts in how I felt and how I was adjusting. It is difficult to explain, but I would wake up one morning and think, "Oh, something's different today. There's been a shift in my thinking, my attitude, my realization, my adjustment, or in my acceptance that this, indeed, is a permanent change in my life. And it's up to me to make the most of it and to be grateful for the happy parts or the good parts or the learning parts and to keep going the way I choose to go." In general, I want to create a happy, fun life. The life I'd imagined I'd be having with Dan is not possible anymore, so it is time to consciously create a life for myself.

It occurred to me that I married young, grew up with Dan, and now I am growing up without him. In the first weeks after his death, at the age of sixty, I had the thought, "Well, I guess I'd better grow up now." My protector, my provider, my person who made the impossible possible is gone. I've got to figure out how to handle situations on my own.

Admittedly, I have done some fumbling and muddling.

I've also become more resourceful and capable in many regards. I have learned to ask for help and to pay for help. I'm pretty pleased in general with how things are now flowing in my life.

Part of my strategy for creating a new life is to be very conscious of what brings me happiness, joy, and pleasure. Also, what does *not* bring me happiness, joy, and pleasure. My aim is to spend more time doing what *does* bring me happiness and less time doing what does not. I give myself permission to take on this approach to life. Sometimes I remind myself that it is all right for me to live this way because it is very easy to get caught up in the "shoulds" of life. I have a saying: "Don't should all over yourself." I make an effort to pay attention to what I do like, what feels good to me, and what doesn't feel good to me as I discover who I want to be and who I'm comfortable being.

Accepting his death...

Every one of us is going through the process of acceptance a little differently. Our relationships are all a little different or a lot different. However, every single person who experiences the loss of a loved one will deal with the loss in her own way. This is a very individual affair.

As far as acceptance goes, I believe I am fairly pragmatic, so I knew Dan was dead and I knew there were certain things that had to be done. In the early days, I think a lot of times we kick into a mode of focusing on what needs to be done and we just do it. I feel that in time, the acceptance of the permanence of death seeps deeper and deeper into our psyche. The permanence of death is a tough concept to accept. It seems that the edges of the thoughts about the permanence of death are really jagged and sharp at first. After some time and some processing, those edges smooth out a bit. I don't think we ever stop missing the person, but I think we start to recognize that its futile to try to bring that person back. As the acceptance settles deeper within us, we can start making different choices for our lives. We can begin to reset our thinking, our perspective on life, the way we view happiness. We also reset our faith in life and in goodness. We make space to focus on shaping our new identity.

In the first few days, weeks, and possibly even months, the veil that separates life and death seems very thin. It seems so thin that many people who have recently lost a loved one have the urge to either pull the loved one back through the veil or, not surprisingly, jump through the veil to join the departed loved one. Either scenario seems entirely possible…for a while. I can't say I wanted to jump to the other side of the veil, but I did notice that the tight grip I had on living in this physical plane loosened a bit. Personally, I have no fear of dying and crossing the veil when the time is upon me. Until then, I am very aware I have many good reasons to remain here. Dan was a big part of my life, a precious and favorite part of my life, but not the only part of my life. I still have children and grandchildren to live for. I still have enough to live for to keep me engaged while here, and I also have a heightened appreciation for the magnificence and fragility of life. Each moment counts.

Grief is a process, and it is not linear. Some days I feel pretty good, and the next day some song or smell or sight triggers a memory and I struggle to keep a smile on my face and tears out of my eyes. I don't ever think I'll get to a point of being happy my husband died, but I do keep a positive and grateful attitude toward life. There is some peace in surrendering and in letting the mind become accustomed to the new reality.

However, it is not for others to tell us where we should be in the grieving process. Grieving is very individual. Each of us must pick, plod, crawl, and dance our way through the field that sometimes leads uphill and sometimes downhill. It is all part of the landscape of our new lives.

JENNIFER

In a way, I don't consider this as creating a new identity but rather a continuation of whatever story I started at my birth. The chapters just keep piling on until they don't. Really, it's just a gradual process for me because I'm still in survival mode from day to day. I need to make sure there's a roof over my family's head, healthy food on the table, and most importantly I need to make sure that I'm raising my children the best way I am able. So, I guess my ever-evolving identity is being created spontaneously—you know, I'm going with the flow and breathing. However, as I look back, I'm beginning to see myself as a stronger person than I ever thought I could be.

It's unimaginable that anyone left alone with an infant and a toddler in such intense grief could possibly come out completely sane. Yep, this so-called insanity I have really is a blessing. I'm learning so much about myself. I am simply a single woman with small people in my life.

I'm hoping I can be a source of comfort and assurance that you're not crazy and that you're stronger than you could ever imagine.

CHAPTER FOURTEEN

And Here Come the Holidays and Anniversaries
Facing the first year of milestones

TRISH

I didn't know how I was going to feel at the time of special holidays and anniversaries, but from all I had heard, the first year can be very difficult, so I made sure I was busy planning the first Celebration of Life near what would have been his next birthday in September, and then the second Celebration of Life in the Chicago area around what would have been our thirty-seventh wedding anniversary.

Thanksgiving was the first major holiday without Bob, and I spent it with our daughter, Räna, and her family. I tried my best to stay in the present moment. However, when I pulled into the driveway at home after the dinner, I smelled a grilling turkey wafting through the air. My mind went into immediate racing mode as I asked myself if this was a sign that Bob was with me or if I'd smelled that turkey because I was about to be a combination of sad and mad at him for not being here to carry on the grilling tradition set in stone for most of our marriage. I couldn't decide in that moment and hurried into the empty house while contemplating. Finally, I decided it was a little of everything and a good night's sleep was in order.

I spent Christmas with my daughter and her in-laws. On the way home, while heading west, I could see dark clouds looming over the horizon as I headed in the direction of my home. I thought the weather was appropriate, as I was returning to an empty house without my husband. Memories of past Christmases flickered through my head: the shopping Bob and I did for the kids; the kids waking up to surprises under the tree; the tradition of lovingly preparing lasagna on Christmas Eve and then the family's anticipation of Bob grilling his masterpiece—marinated flank steak—on Christmas. I could feel the tears building up and my throat constricting, but as I turned south with the Sandia Mountains to the east, I caught sight of a most gorgeous start of the sunset. Yes, New Mexico is known for 360-degree sunsets! Clouds and sky were ablaze in deep orange, gold, pink, deep blues and purple. I knew, without hesitation, that it was a sign from Bob saying he was still with me. That, in itself, was comforting.

As a whole family, we decided to celebrate two days after Christmas in Durango, Colorado, and treat the kids and grandkids to a ride on the Polar Express train. My son Justin's in-laws joined us, and we had a marvelous time watching the youngsters have a blast on the train. It was easy to stay in the moment. On the following ten-degree and bitterly cold day, we strolled throughout the quaint downtown area before heading home. With some arm twisting, my daughter finally convinced me to venture into one of the stores we had walked past earlier. A familiar object caught my eye toward the back of the store—a framed, large, iridescent blue butterfly just like the one Bob bought for me at the Chicago history museum years ago that had faded badly over the years from the intense New Mexico sunlight. He'd always wanted to replace it, but we never knew where to get a new one. Well, there it was! It was definitely a gift from Bob and once again, it takes its rightful place in the house. I smile every time I pass by it.

Then the day of love arrived. I knew I didn't want to spend Valentine's Day in my home alone, so I decided to make it a special day with my then five-year-old grandson, Kade, at the Albuquerque Bio Park. We shared a pizza in a cozy restaurant following the outing. Then it was back to my house for an overnight treat of movies and popcorn. It was easy to focus all my thoughts on the delightful time together with my pint-sized Valentine!

On the first anniversary date of his passing we, as a family, couldn't do the two things Bob loved—a train ride or a baseball game. A train ride to Santa Fe meant we were going to have to deal with a standing-room-only train and huge crowds gathered for the Indian Market. The baseball team was out of town that weekend. I stayed home that day and wrote in my journal, reflecting on all the ways I've grown since Bob passed on. It was a very cathartic exercise, and I was pleased with all the ways I had already adapted to the many changes in my life. I was also pleased with my new identity, which was taking form.

In year two, the family expanded once again. After two back-to-back miscarriages, with the first miscarriage happening during Bob's passing and the second miscarriage happening around the following first Christmas, Räna gave birth to an adorable healthy baby boy just eight days shy of my birthday in March. Life has gotten very full again, and a new routine is starting to take form. Life changes, and so have I. I've chosen to reflect on how far I've come since Bob passed on August 21, 2014. I'm happily accumulating new memories with each passing holiday, anniversary, and now a birth that demonstrates that the cycle of life continues. I will always have the past memories, and I'm delighted to report that the sad emotions they used to bring are beginning to soften.

PEGGY

As the date rolls around each year, I am aware of it. I'm aware of it for weeks leading up to the date. Dan happened to die on my parents' wedding anniversary and eleven days after our wedding anniversary. Also, our anniversaries straddle Valentine's Day…lots of love. It is a special time of year for many reasons. I do make an effort to do something pleasant on that day. I didn't want to turn the dates sour for myself or for anyone else. I have fought the urge to connect with our sons and remind them, "This is the day Dad died." I thought if they could go on about their lives and not feel sad on that date every year, that was a good thing. As it has turned out, by the end of the day each one has reached out to me to let me know he is thinking of Dad and me. The "boys" are very sweet. They know how to share love with me on that day. They recount happy, shared memories and let me know they are proud of me for how I am handling the grieving process and creating a new life chapter.

For Dan's birthday this year, I went to a local park with my friend Debi and released a couple helium-filled balloons that we had attached our handwritten love notes to. The notes expressed our love and appreciation of Dan. The physical body goes away, but the love in our hearts and minds remain. It was nice to have a little ceremonial reminder that I can celebrate his life and my love for him. Debi filmed a short video as I released the balloons, and I shared it with my sons, sisters, and close friends. On other birthdays, I've raised my glass and thought about him.

Feeling celebratory has been a challenge, especially in the first couple years. I do make an effort for my grandchildren at Christmas. I've scaled down my decorating, so setting it all up and taking it all down does not feel so burdensome it squashes all joy. It has been nice that Kyle has continued his family's tradition of hosting brunch. My celebrations are a combination of longstanding traditions and first-time adventures.

The first Dan-less Christmas, Kyle insisted he help me put up Christmas lights on the house. It was important to Kyle that my house not look dark and sad through the first holiday season. I really appreciated his help since my energy was still too low to have enough enthusiasm to handle the task on my own. I was just going to let the idea go and not have lights that year. I'd given myself permission to do what felt right and manageable and not sweat what didn't get done. It was Kyle to the rescue, for which I am very grateful.

In subsequent years as my energy has grown, I've gotten on the roof to put the Christmas lights up by myself. Luckily, we have a southwestern-style house with a flat roof and I can manage the job quite safely.

Yesterday, I was just listening to a book written by a woman who lost her husband. She had a brilliant idea. She proposed to her children who were still living at home, "Let's take two years off from celebrating the way we used to and in the third year we will recreate a new way to celebrate." The children agreed, and the idea worked for the family. I can identify with the wisdom in that mother's thinking. Be willing to embrace change and give yourself permission to do things differently.

My widow friends and I are sensitive and thoughtful when an anniversary or other special date is approaching. We call or text each other and sometimes make lunch, dinner, or travel plans to keep the woman pleasantly occupied for the day. We raise our glasses or dedicate a sunset to the late spouse. We end on a happy note before returning to our respective homes.

JENNIFER

Chuck chose to leave on a memorable day so no one would forget it. Yes, Christmas Eve. Yeah, thank you babe for not leaving on Christmas Day. You know, it just all feels so surreal anyway. So no, I haven't done anything special to mark the day except to light a candle at Christmas in his memory.

CHAPTER FIFTEEN

‐‐‐‐‐‐‐‐‐‐‐‐‐‐‐‐‐‐‐‐‐WW‐‐‐‐‐‐‐‐‐‐‐‐‐‐‐‐‐‐‐

Odd Coincidences
Quirky connections in life and death

TRISH

My mother passed away in 2013, Bob in 2014, and my father 4.5 months later. Whew! With all three deaths being so close together, I learned how different it feels to lose a parent compared to losing a spouse. Truly, they are as different as apples and oranges. I realize my new source of strength is from within!

PEGGY

It seems that quite often deaths happen in multiples. Decades ago, I observed that when a baby is born into our circle, it is not uncommon for another person in our circle to leave the planet. I observed this occurrence often enough as a teenager to develop a saying: "One comes in, one goes out." Two days before Dan died, my sister's grandson was born. My last communication with Dan was a text message: "Mom and baby are healthy and well." He texted back, "That's wonderful!" I didn't realize when the baby was born, it would be my husband who was going.

Dan and I had been caregivers for Dan's ninety-three-year-old Aunt Jenny whom we loved. As dementia got stronger, caring for her became tougher. It is not uncommon for the elder to treat the caregiver badly. That is what happened in our case. We continued to treat her with utmost care and respect, and I was on duty twenty-four hours a day until the day I kissed her on the forehead after she was pronounced dead. One month later, my friend died by suicide. This was a horrible surprise. It hit me hard. Six months later another close friend died suddenly of a heart attack. Another blow. Three months later, Dan died. Good golly! Four deaths in ten months! It seems that many times deaths come in clusters. There is no time to recover or adjust to one before the next happens. Quick! Take a breath and move forward.

JENNIFER

There are so many things that can be an odd coincidence. I believe in synchronicity, the little things that lead into those bigger, "Oh, so that's what that meant," type of ah-ha events. We should always be open to the subtleties of the universe because it is always leading us along our paths.

I don't know if I ever really thought that much about co-incidences relating to life and death, but I sure did have a lot of deaths in a row. First it was Chuck, followed shortly after by my mother, and then my dearest Aunt Rushia Mae, who passed on due to old age. I just believe they all belonged to the same soul group and they are traveling together.

CHAPTER SIXTEEN

---WW---

Looking at the Bright Side of Being a Widow
Focusing on what we **do** have rather than on what we **don't** have

TRISH

It struck me one day that being called Mrs. Comer at twenty-two felt stranger than being referred to as a widow at fifty-eight. Perhaps it was a sign of maturity and wisdom.

To me, being a widow has been a gradual process of denial and acceptance through a series of daily and monthly changes. I still allow myself to feel sad and grieve when sadness arrives, and then I allow the sadness to pass.

However, being a widow is not the end of the world, but a start to new beginnings. I feel I have been given an opportunity to create a new identity and to start a new and very different chapter in the second half of my life. I am grateful for this time. I choose to be as open and receptive as I can about all the wonders and opportunities this world offers. I choose to allow more beauty, love, peace, health, and prosperity to enter into my life as I strive for harmony and balance.

On a more humorous side note, I no longer need to compromise on where we go to dinner or what to watch on TV. Those decisions, at least for the time being, are all mine now!

PEGGY

The first time I was called a widow, I felt a degree of shock. The word couldn't apply to me, heck no. But yes, it did. That drove the harsh reality home. It wasn't an insult, it wasn't a cause for a pity party, it was just a new title that I had not invited into my life at that time. There I was wearing the new title. It's true, I can't argue with it. I am a widow. I did outlive my husband. It hits when I go into a doctor's office and on the form I check a box under the heading, Marital Status. My gosh, for forty-two years I'd checked Married. Now I'm checking Widow. It's something new to adjust to. It's not a horrible thing. It is what it is. Also, under the heading Sex, I now check No or Not Anymore, which is a joke. Most forms use the word Sex instead of Gender, so why not have some fun?

Being a widow means going through a huge adjustment in all aspects of life. Being a widow means being kind to one's self, it means taking the time and energy to nurture one's self, because becoming a widow is not an easy undertaking. Being a widow takes energy. I've often commented, "We spent all those years learning to live together, and then all of a sudden we have to spend years learning to live without the other."

It's a tough transition. There are a lot of details that go into taking on widowhood. Dan and I had some of our paperwork prepared but not all. That was coming in two weeks, after we had unpacked and moved into our new home for a few weeks. Having that paperwork done and decisions made is all very helpful. I don't think it serves anyone to avoid discussions about the inevitable. It is difficult enough to deal with the pain and sadness of losing a spouse without having to also search though papers, make phone calls, and take care of a lot of business details. I say, face facts, have discussions, make decisions, and get paperwork legally prepared. Attorneys' fees today can make tomorrow much brighter.

There comes a time to move forward, focus on what remains, and express gratitude and appreciation. We look forward to the goodness and joy we will create. In the early days, every day can feel like a challenge. Eventually, every day feels more like a gift.

JENNIFER

I recall the first time I was referred to as a widow. It felt shocking, weird, and surreal. It felt as though someone was lying to me. I think of much older women being called widows, not the young woman I am. Well, it is what it is. So, typically I don't refer to myself as a widow unless it's to thwart off an unwanted advance from a man. Being defined as a widow is the same as having an unwanted notch in my belt! It's a story lost and a new story gained. Life goes on differently, but it's always going to be of my choosing, just as your life is going to be of your choosing.

I don't know if there are any real benefits of being a widow due to my age and circumstances. There are not many that I can see. Being single now with all the responsibilities has been a tough journey that surely would have been easier with a partner at my side. However, it's been full of lessons and opportunities to learn how to be resourceful, adaptable, and flexible. Being a widow is not like being divorced. There are no days with Dad. Every decision from here on out is solely mine, so the only benefits of my being a single woman that I can see, and yes, it is really a small thing in the grand scheme of things, is when it comes to home decorating. I must confess, this part has been fun.

CHAPTER SEVENTEEN

Our Children and Grandchildren
Their thoughts…

Räna Comer Doyal—Age 38, Trish's daughter

My dad and I were very close. We had an exemplary father-daughter bond. As a child, my dad was the only one who I would let teach me anything. He taught me how to ride a bike, dress myself, tie my shoes. He was patient with me, and I was patient with him. He knew the importance of teaching me how to change tires, oil, and spark plugs. He even went out to Sears and bought me my very own toolbox the day I moved out of my parents' house. He wanted to make sure I was always taken care of and if not, that I could take care of myself.

My dad and I had this special way to communicate, often with a raise of the eyebrows or a silly smile, and we would both start laughing. He was always someone I could talk to, and he never forgot if he did or said something to upset me. Even when I was an overly sensitive hormonal teenager, my dad would sit me down to talk about our disagreement and we would both apologize. Even if it was for something he said or did years ago, my dad would pull me aside and say, "I should've said it then, but I'm sorry." He was an easy man to forgive and to ask for forgiveness. He was an eternal source of unconditional love.

My dad has been gone for two and a half years now. I was thirty-five when he died. I feel thirty-five is a young age to lose a parent, but losing a parent at the age of thirty-five is not necessarily as life-altering as losing a parent at a young age, when the loss forever sculpts who the child will become because their quintessence of self is still tacky and hasn't quite set all the way. Even so, I thought my dad would meet my children someday and be the grandpa to them that mine was to me. I thought I would get to watch my parents grow old together and develop stereotypical nuances and eccentricities that plague older folks, like cranking the heat up in the winter and sporting socks with sandals.

Not that there should be an acceptable age to accept death, but in our society, there kind of is. There is this perception that once we reach a certain age, life should be pretty much wrapped up. Goals should have been met, family enjoyed, memories preserved, grievances forgiven. It's not always so neatly packaged for everyone, but I feel if we keep telling ourselves this, then it makes it easier to process.

Sixty years old is not an acceptable age to accept death. I don't really know what that particular age is for myself personally, but when I lost my grandfather just four and a half months after my dad, things were made a bit clearer. My grandpa was an amazing man and I felt great sadness knowing I would never be able to see him again, but I also felt a sense of peace. My grandpa missed my grandma, who had died two years earlier. He'd had a pretty great life, and he was surrounded by lots of family who adored him. He was a proud man with an unmeasurable amount of love, and he was fulfilled. I was able to process and accept his death a bit more simply and with ease. Of course, my bond with my grandpa was different and perhaps not as close as the bond I shared with my dad, but my grandfather was also twenty-five years older than my dad. Would it have been easier to lose my dad twenty-five years from now? I will never really know.

So no, my dad's death still does not sit well with me. He had dreams he hadn't touched, or perhaps they were the dreams I wanted for him. I wanted my dad to become a published author. I wanted to see my mom and him retire in Hawaii. I wanted him to take another long walk unannounced and return home with a brand new pickup truck. I had always pictured my mom and dad frequenting the patios of local restaurants for early dinners and continuing their philosophical or transcendental chit chat as they occasionally discuss how every child that walks by reminds them of their own grandkids, though not as cute or not as clever, of course. I still cannot process that when I celebrated my dad's sixtieth birthday, it was going to be the last one, especially with so many lingering regrets.

I learned of my dad's death as I laid in pain and heartbreak on my couch while I was in the middle of losing my first child due to a miscarriage. It was the one day I didn't spend at the hospital, and it was the same day my dad left. This particular day came with no do overs or second chances, and that consumed me for days, weeks, and even months after his passing. But in time, as with everything else, I came to believe my aunt Ann, who was also there every single day, when she told me that it was because of our special bond that my dad couldn't leave in my presence. He didn't want to die in front of me. Once the cloud of self-inflicted guilt lifted, my head believed that to be true and eventually my heart did, too.

How do our children see us? How do they view our process?

There was a very short time when my dad was still with me and my family and when we had finally accepted that he was going to die. It was during this time my mom became distant with me, withdrawn, and quiet. At times, she treated me rather uncharacteristically unkindly. At the time, this hurt me and made me somewhat irritated with her treatment, but I quickly recognized it was not to be taken personally. We had all just learned that my dad was going to die. Just prior to that, we were all told that he would be fine and within the next nine days, my dad had died. My mom had to say goodbye to her true love and support system of thirty-six years within those next nine days. I cannot fathom what that should or could feel like, nor do I think that there is any right or wrong way to process saying goodbye. My mom was doing the best she could to hold herself together during those moments, and who was I to judge how she was holding herself together?

At first it was really difficult to understand or even try to process what my mom was going through. I was dealing with my own grief for both my dad and the baby I lost. I tried to be there for my mom, but it was very difficult to get past my own fears, feelings, and denial. I hurt for my mom. I would try to imagine how suddenly alone she felt now that this huge presence, support system, and the man who not only shared her life but had become her most integral partner was just suddenly gone. I wanted to be there for my mom and at the time, I really thought I was. On August 21, 2014, my husband held me in his arms while I struggled to comprehend that I was miscarrying my baby and my dad had just died. I felt excruciating pain and numb at the same time. I felt anguish and love at the same time. But I did not feel alone. I had my husband's strong arms wrapped tightly around me as my tears soaked through his shirt. I had someone to sob to and sob with. We could cry together for the loss of our baby as well as the loss of both of our fathers. We held each other up. On August 21, 2014, my mom no longer had that. It broke my heart, and there's no way I could even begin to imagine how that would feel or how she should handle it.

After my dad passed, it seemed like almost immediately–though I'm sure it wasn't–my mom gave away a lot of my dad's belongings to us kids. Though it was mostly clothing, I remember being somewhat stung by these actions. I felt quick to snatch up whatever I could of my dad's and hold it close as though I could hug him through his Hawaiian shirts and my memories. Some of his shirts and jackets even still smelled like him and that made me feel like he was still here with me. I couldn't understand why my mom wouldn't want to cling to that too. But when I think back to that time now, I can see just how painful it must be to have my dad's belongings teasingly smelling like him. His belongings must have made it seem like he was still close to being in this world, yet he was really gone. It must be difficult to be a part of that dance, to have your senses tell you that he's still here, but your head tell you otherwise.

During this time, I was also worried about my mom. I was worried about her being alone in the house she had shared with my dad for twenty-five years. It was the house we grew up in. It was the house that held our memories, our growing pains and our countless birthdays celebrated with the Beatles playing in the background. And she was alone at night in this house, engulfed by her memories and her silent thoughts with no one there to tell her it would all be okay. I would check up on her and she would always tell me she was okay whether that was the truth or not. She would share with me dreams she had of my dad or conversations she'd experienced. Really, I wanted to give her the time she needed, but at the same time I worried endlessly about how slow time was moving for her and for myself. Perhaps by giving her time, I was also giving her space. Was it too much space? Before this, I hadn't really lost anyone so close to me that it would impact my life. I had lost great grandparents as a child and both grandmas, but I'd had a lot of time to process their deaths before they actually died. My dad's loss was so sudden and so momentous, I didn't know what to do. I didn't know what to do with myself, and I especially didn't know the right thing to do for my mom. So I let her do what she needed to do—no questions asked, no judgments passed. I just made sure she knew I was there for her. I was never sure if that was the best thing to do for my mom, but it was all I could do.

My mom has come a long way in the past two and a half years. She seems much more peaceful now, though I'm sure there remain tough days. There certainly are for me, so I can only imagine how much more difficult it is for her—especially when a Pink Floyd song comes on, or the St. Louis Cardinals are mentioned, or even just when she hears a simple train whistle.

After the first year of my dad's passing, I mentioned dating to my mom. I wasn't sure when she would be ready, but I wanted her to know that I was very supportive of this. I know she has taken steps toward perhaps just thinking about dating someone else, but she seems to hold back and understandably so. My dad still holds her heart, and he always will. But it is lonely when you have so much more life to live and experiences to transpire and no one to share that with. I know there is no replacement for my dad, nor do I want that, but I would like to see my mom with someone who makes her happy and I know someday she will find that.

I didn't have any kids before my dad died—something that, from time to time, creeps across my heart and still haunts me. And with that, I consider this subject a two-part regret. The first part being that my son will never know my dad. I suppose that's one of the hardest parts for me to cope with after the two and a half years he's been gone. My grandpa was a remarkable and influential man. It saddens me greatly when I think about how my son will never meet him. It is overwhelmingly worse when I think about how my son will never meet my dad. My husband lost his father the same year I lost mine. It really tugs at my heart to know that my son won't ever meet his grandfathers and have the potentially same sweet relationships that I had.

The second part is that my dad will never know my son. As children, we often want to share our successes with our parents. We value their approval and praise. It can make us feel proud. I don't think that ever goes away as we grow into adults, but perhaps just evolves. Instead of sharing with our parents soccer trophies or A+ papers, we now want to share the homes we have built, jobs we have secured, and the children we have brought into this world. A moment doesn't go by when I don't wish I could say, "See, Dad, look at this little life I have created. See how he has your eyes!" And well, he does—my son has my eyes, and I have my dad's. There will be times that my son will make a face or give a look that completely embodies my dad and it absolutely fills my soul because it feels like, for just a moment, I can see my dad in my son and then just maybe, they aren't complete strangers after all.

Justin Comer – Age 36, Trish's son

The timing of my dad's passing was shocking. He went from dealing with what we thought was a possible minor illness to dying three-and-a-half months later. It was so fast that it was hard to wrap my head around it, especially since my daughter Kylah was born about three weeks before.

I remember the day Kylah was born. I wanted to share the exciting and happy news with him. I only had to drive just a couple of blocks from where she was born to the other hospital where my dad had his first of two hospital stays. As soon as I saw him, I just had the feeling he wasn't going to make it. It was difficult to compartmentalize my feelings. The moment was very bittersweet—my daughter had just been born, and maybe my dad was getting ready to pass away.

Originally, when my mom asked us to bring Kylah to their house to see my dad for the first time, the timing of her request conflicted with other plans, but my wife Sheena told me, "We need to go. He needs to see her. I just feel we need to do this." Call it a premonition on her part, but in hindsight, I'm really thankful she convinced me to change our plans so he could see her the one and only time.

The last picture we have of my dad is of him holding Kylah in his arms. At the time we took the picture, I had this feeling there was some kind of meaning behind my newborn daughter's arrival and the possibility that my dad would be departing soon after. It was a strangely eerie and fleeting feeling, and I didn't want to believe it, so I tried to put it out of my mind. However, while watching the slideshow that my sister put together for our dad's celebration of life a month later, I noticed she had chosen the picture of my dad holding Kylah as the last picture in the slideshow. It was then I knew my feelings had been correct.

I believe what helped me take my mind off of his passing the most was having a very demanding job and a growing family of three kids and a newborn baby. However, I didn't allow myself the time to grieve in the beginning. That didn't come until a year or so later.

My dad's departure left a hole in my heart, and to make matters worse, I lost my Gramps four-and-a-half months later. Both were my rocks. I could count on them for their guidance, and now they were gone. However, those two deaths forced me to question and evaluate where I was at in my own life and all the changes I saw that I needed to make to become the stronger person I am today. The hardest part was dealing with my emotions and thoughts alone. Emotionally, I felt I was living all alone on an island.

There's so much I miss about my dad, but what I miss the most is not having my essential male role model in my life. I learned so much from him during all the years I was growing up. There are many things I do as a father, spouse, and homeowner that I have learned from my dad.

There are some things I wish I could hear his opinion about. I know he was proud of me, as he had told me on many past occasions, so I know wherever he is that he is proud of what I have accomplished and will continue to accomplish.

I try not to live with regrets in my life, but I wish I could have known him better, not just as a father, but as a person. I wish I could have a conversation with him as the person I am now because I understand myself better than I did even a few years ago. He was a wonderful grandpa, and I do wish the kids would have had a chance to get to know him better now that they are older.

There are good memories I will always have, and my fondest memories are about the one-on-one time we used to spend together. He was my Little League baseball coach up until high school, and the both of us practiced at a local park many times. There was the time just the two of us drove to Denver for a Cubs/Rockies baseball game when I was in high school. It was a fun road trip and even though the Cubbies lost, we had lots of laughs and time to really get to know one another better.

We mostly camped as a family, but one time in particular, he and I went with our dog, Boomer, to camp in the Mogollon Range in Arizona. Originally, we had planned on meeting my dad's childhood buddy and his two younger boys, but we completely missed seeing them because we got distracted by a young boy demonstrating his fly fishing skills to his father on the side of the road. The young boy accidentally threw the rod into the road and my dad accidentally drove over it. The boy's timing couldn't have been worse, but apparently, it was meant to be because after that it just ended up being a very interesting trip with just the two of us and our dog.

On the way back, The VLRs (Very Large Arrays—deep space listening devices), which are normally visible a ways off from the road, went by in a blink! Our dog ate too many leftover hot dogs back at the campsite, and we broke speed records just so we could drive fast enough with the windows rolled down to keep the smell out of the car! And we didn't get stopped by the state police! We had so many good talks and so many good laughs. I will cherish those memories forever. I wonder what fond memories my children will have of me when they become adults.

I was asked about how we children see our mothers and how we view their process.

Since I've never lost a spouse, I could only guess how she was feeling, but I could see she was trying to be strong for the family. At times I wondered if she was trying to convince herself that she needed to be strong.

My mom has come a long way in becoming her own person. Now I can see her strength and the strength it took her to write this book. I know it couldn't have been easy, but I sense it was a part of her healing. I can see that sharing her feelings, experiences, and thoughts with the other co-writers can provide support for those who will read this book. This book also shows how each person has their own unique challenges but coming together and talking can really help the healing process. It's good for us kids to see how our mothers handled it so that if the day comes when we may need to deal with the loss of a spouse, we have an example of how to heal.

Our grandchildren…

Our grandchildren were very sad, but our five-year-old

grandson, Kade, had the most insight. He asked his dad—my son, Justin—if they could go see "Bobba" at the mortuary. Justin patiently explained to him that his body would be there, but his spirit has gone on and left the world as we know it. Just to be sure Kade understood what he would see at the mortuary, Justin asked him once again if he really wanted to go, but Kade still insisted to see Bobba one more time and he said he wanted everyone to wear their team sport shirts since Bobba was a big fan of the St. Louis Cardinal's baseball team and the Chicago Bears football team. We all showed up dressed as requested. It was actually very cute, and it lightened the moment. The kids, including my son's stepchildren, approached his body and were surprisingly very calm and subdued. My worst fear, that they would freak out, was laid to rest.

I've asked Kade on occasion if he still thinks about Bobba. He said he does, and that Bobba has been in his dreams.

PEGGY

Kyle—age 42, Peggy's son

I lost my father when I was in my late thirties and well into being a father myself. Although I was no longer directly dependent on him on a daily basis, I was still quite dependent on him for advice on life's challenges. He was also my best friend, and one of the few people who had a deep and accurate understanding of me. It's that loss that I still feel every day. Many things I would share with him I now have no one to share with. Whenever I am missing Dad a lot, I make a pot of green chile stew his style.

Dad's death was tragic, lamentable, inevitable, and irreversible. Knowing that has helped me not get stuck in the sorrow of the loss.

My view of my mother has changed dramatically since his death. She always had her strengths, and no one would ever have thought her frail, but she has shown courage and strength in areas I had never seen before. If anything, it has made us closer and deepened my appreciation for her to see her bear up bravely under the weight of this loss and the life changes it has precipitated.

My children, Kiera and Rhys, were in early elementary school when my father passed away. They had a very good, loving relationship with him and saw him frequently. When he died, we made a great effort not to sugarcoat anything and to give them complete answers to their questions. They had previously been exposed to death only through the passing of pets, but they had at least gotten that chance to understand the permanence of death. Our approach has been to shift their attention to the wonderful impact he had on their lives, as opposed to focusing on lamenting his passing, as we believe this is a healthier perspective. He still comes up in conversations regularly with them now, years removed from his death, and always when referencing happy memories.

Our grandchildren…

Our granddaughter Kiera was six, and our grandson Rhys was three.

I was out of town when Dan fell off the ladder inside the house. I was not present when the children were told. I arrived the next day.

Kyle and family had stopped by our new home hours before the fall. They were the last family members to see Dan alive.

I imagine the children were told pretty much early on since their dad, our son Kyle, is very practical. He and his wife, Erin, went to the hospital right away and they must have left the children with Erin's mother, who lives nearby. The grandchildren were most likely told Opa was hurt before their parents left for the hospital. When Kyle and Erin returned to the children, they probably explained that the situation was serious and Opa was not coming home. After five years, we still have not talked about all the details of the day. I'm still learning little tidbits from friends and family from time to time.

The grandchildren had some experience with the death of pets, which in hindsight was probably helpful. Kiera was precious. While adults were buzzing around my house making arrangements for the service, writing the obituary, and keeping everyone fed, Kiera found arts and crafts materials in my office and created a beautiful card that read, "We miss Opa, too." The inside of the card was illustrated with a garden sprinkling can that was showering a row of heart-shaped flowers below. Inside the card read, "Sprinkle love in your heart." I will cherish that card forever.

We encouraged both grandchildren to talk about Opa and ask questions freely. We answered truthfully and appropriately for their ages. One day when Rhys was four, he made up a song about Opa and amazed me with his insight about love, death, and spirit. That is a moment I wish had been recorded.

Both grandchildren seem to have accepted the death of Opa and view it as a part of the life cycle. Every once in a while, one or the other will say, "I miss Opa." We agree, talk about

Opa for a few minutes and go on with our activity.

Noah—age 33, Peggy's son

If you continue to think the way you used to think, you'll constantly be thinking about him. Everything will remind you of him, and you'll be sad all the time. So instead, you learn to change how you think in order to continue with life. It's not denial and you're not attempting to forget. It's just that thinking about him all the time gets in the way of the life you still have. So, you discipline yourself. You learn to control the memories to be able to decide when to allow all the things that remind you of him to make you sad. However, it requires a constant discipline and it changes how you think.

A recent text message from Noah to Peggy: Thinking of you momma! I love you and I'm so proud of you for how you have persevered and for what you have made of your life.

Losing a loved one, someone on whom you depend, throws you into an alternate reality where you are forced to go on living without them. Each day, you are reminded of the ways your life would be different and better if they were still alive. You feel that you belong in that original timeline, that you are not equipped to survive in this one.

But there is no way back. For some time, this life feels horribly broken, as if a psychic limb has been cruelly ripped from you. You limp along without hope of joy. At some point, though, you begin to realize that you can still be happy. This loss doesn't erase everything. Slowly, you learn to make do without that limb.

You aren't made whole. That wound is still there. That limb is still gone. But you learn to modify your thinking. Again, it's not denial and you're not attempting to forget. It's just that thinking about them all the time gets in the way of the life you still have, so you discipline yourself. Unbidden memories no longer stop you in your tracks.

There may be more to this process. Perhaps there is a lasting healing at the end of it. I'm not there yet.

Birk—age 31, Peggy's son

I was asked to talk about how the death of my father in 2012 has affected me as well as my observations of how my mom has dealt with the situation.

If you are reading this because you find yourself in a similar situation, my condolences to you and your loved ones.

First of all, I guess I have been putting this off as long as possible because this makes me think about things I got really good at suppressing. Some might say I have a dim look on situations like these but one of the things I have learned is it doesn't matter how you look at it, it will always suck.

I guess I should explain who my father was to me. He was everything. You knew that if he was around, everything was all right, even if it wasn't. I feel like I'd barely scratched the surface of the knowledge and wisdom he kept up in his head, and it is now forever lost. This feeling of loss is not something I can shake, and I have realized I will never be able to.

There is no healing from losing a parent. Time passes and it gets easier to avoid thinking about it, but there will always be things that remind you that they are gone and it will hurt just as much as the first day. In my opinion, there is only one thing you can do. *Keep going.* Life won't wait for you. If you want to keep that person alive, honor him by making yourself better. Take the things you admired about him most and make it a part of you.

Right, so how has Mom handled the situation? I would have to say she has dealt with it in the best way. She kept going! She never once turned to alcohol or drugs, which would have made things worse on everyone else. Now if you know Peggy and you are reading this you are probably thinking, "Of course she never turned to drugs or alcohol. She never did those in the first place." I feel like it's important to mention this for everyone's sake. Drugs and alcohol will only impede the egregious emotions you need to wade through in order to eventually feel somewhat normal again.

It's hard for me to remember how Mom handled life without Dad the first couple of years because I was in the Navy at the time and was only home for nine days after Dad died. Then I had to return to my duty station over a thousand miles away and on a submarine, where I had no contact for months at a time. When I could, I would spend many hours talking to Mom on the phone which, hopefully, helped her get back to feeling somewhat normal after such a big loss.

I guess the best way I can explain how Mom dealt with it was a lot like how a train gets going. It takes a lot of power to turn the wheels at first, and in some instances the wheels lose traction, but they keep turning in the right direction. After the train reaches a certain speed, none of the wheels lose traction anymore and the train continues to increase speed until there is no stopping it. After Dad died, Mom had to figure out all the bills, taxes, car care, house repair, and everything else Dad took care of. In the past five years, Mom has really shown her ability to adapt and overcome. She got a handle on the things that were taken care of by Dad and most importantly, she has continued to live her life. She takes care of her health. She tends her business and earns an income to support herself. She spends time with family and friends. She travels and has fun. I am very proud of her.

JENNIFER

My son was just a month into his fourth year when Chuck died. A child that age doesn't understand time yet. His awareness of death is just now starting to take hold. There's a lot of anger surfacing right now. I feel I often get the blame for not being able to fulfill the masculine requirements his father would have fulfilled. Charlie Anne is just now old enough that I can actually leave the house without the fear of losing one of them.

I often tear up when I think about how little Hayden was when Chuck left while I was still pregnant with Charlie Anne. Some strange, out-of-the-blue thoughts came to me during those last few weeks and days Chuck was still here in this plane. Who will protect us? Who will walk Charlie Anne down the aisle when she gets married? Who will ever love them the way he would have? I know there will never be a "perfect" replacement of him. However, I hope I will find a love that's comparable, a lover who will honor Chuck and love us the way Chuck would have. If not, it is what it is, and we will just keep riding the rainbow.

CHAPTER EIGHTEEN

Where Do I See Myself In One Year?
New horizons ahead

TRISH

I've learned much since Bob passed on. I've learned how to be more resilient and flexible than I had ever been before. I learned that being able to forgive and be more loving opens my heart to receive more love. I learned having gratitude brings me more experiences to be grateful for. I am learning who I am as I continue to develop my new identity. I've learned to clear away the cobwebs from the past in order to create a clean slate on which to build a new life. Ultimately, I learned that joy, peace, happiness, and well-being lies solely in my own hands.

My outlook on life has changed since Bob passed on. Now, life to me is like a coloring book, and I've come to an understanding that there will always be parts to my new identity that I haven't yet colored in. Instead of a box of eight crayons, I see myself as having a box of sixty-four. I ask myself, "What picture will I color this year? What colors will I choose?"

Currently, I've taken all sixty-four crayons out of the box and laid them on the table. Beautiful shades of blue, green, yellow and red lie there for my choosing. I've chosen to color in a page that includes the publication of my manuscript on harmony and balance.

On the horizon, I see myself offering workshops about healing grief and publishing a blog that will be used as a platform where stories can be shared that can inspire others to heal and be supportive of one another on their healing journey.

I see more traveling just because I love exploring and learning about new places, cultures, and the people that live in those places.

I see being with my soul mate. I see us happy, loving, and content with one another. I see us traveling or just happy while sitting on the couch holding hands. I have so much love to give and so much love to receive, as does he.

Ultimately, I see my soul continuing to evolve. I see my harmony and balance message being refined and shared with the world.

I hear myself saying to others, "You, too, can heal. You, too, can thrive. You, too, can love once again. You, too, can re-establish harmony and balance in your heart and in your life. You may not know this now, but you, too, have a box of sixty-four crayons, or maybe more. Life can be limited to eight crayons or life can be unlimited with as many crayons in as many shades of colors as you like. It's your choice!"

PEGGY

Where do I see myself in one year? I see myself with more energy and more of an ability to think, focus, and celebrate.

I feel that my energy will flow even more smoothly, my thoughts will be clearer, and making decisions will be easier because I will have become accustomed to a new way of making decisions. I expect to be by myself, in this home that we built together. I'm leaving the door open for new and wonderful adventures and events. Emotionally, I expect to be in a good spot. I think I've gone through many of the hardest parts. Those first couple of years were very tough. I felt like an elephant was sitting on my chest, squeezing my heart. Later, it felt more like a load of bricks. Over time, and with every shift, the weight became a little lighter and then a little lighter still. The pressure that was squeezing my heart eased a bit. In the first days and weeks, smiling and laughing were pretty difficult. I remember purchasing groceries and trying to smile and chat with the cashier. Nope, it wasn't happening. My facial muscles just wouldn't cooperate. Thank goodness that has changed. I find it much easier to smile these days. That feels good. I anticipate that will continue to be even easier a year from now.

People like to say, "Time heals all wounds." Actually, I believe it is *what we do* with that time that matters and encourages healing. I expect to be in an even better place emotionally in a year because I am taking conscious steps to get there. I've become very aware of my energy and how it's spent. I am also very discerning about the energy I allow to come into my space and the people I choose to have around me. It has been important to be in contact with people who have a positive outlook on life in general as well as people who are understanding and who allow me to move through my process at my own pace.

In a year I will have a few more adventures under my belt.

In March 2017, my friend Estelle and I traveled to Madikwe Game Reserve, Thakadu River Camp, South Africa on a photo safari. This was the trip of a lifetime! Being in the wild, just feet from beautiful and powerful lions, cheetahs, elephants, and zebras was breathtaking. A peace came over me while on this trip that lingers to this day. The trip was hosted by our friends Tricia and Kevin Dooley of Idube Photo Safaris (www.idubephotosafaris.com). They saw to our every need, comfort and safety. This was important because Estelle, widowed about two years after me, and I were on this big adventure without our husbands/protectors.

One year from now I will continue to honor Dan's memory by living a whole, content, and joyful life. I will take advantage of opportunities to be with our children and grandchildren. I will continue to express my love and appreciation for my family. I will remember the good times Dan and I shared, and I will remember the wisdoms learned in our forty-two years together. With every breath, I will appreciate the gift of life.

As humans, we have the opportunity to experience many emotions. These opportunities are varied, and the emotions vary from feel-good emotions to painful emotions. As we travel along our paths, we develop understanding and compassion.

Because of my experience of losing the love of my life in an unexpected instant, I recently shared heartfelt sentiment with my precious niece April and her husband Michael, who were marking the sixth month after their newborn son passed away. I said, "And we carry on with a new chapter in life, letting our tough life experiences grow our compassion and understanding. Never fully 'recovering,' we learn to walk side-by-side with our sorrow as well as the wisdom and joy it gives us opportunity to savor."

Making this a strength-discovery adventure rather than an unfortunate burden life has dealt me is a conscious choice. I am determined to learn to walk through this tough time and come out able to feel joy again. So, in a year I will experience more joy.

JENNIFER

That's a tough question for me to answer at the moment since I'm focused on keeping both feet on the ground and moving forward with my life. Now that both of my kids are at school, I'm starting to look at possibilities or make opportunities where there were none even just a year ago. I stay in a daydream-like world where I'm free of overwhelming responsibilities, free of the loneliness and the grief. I can see myself with someone who loves me and my children dearly and who has a stable income so I can be free to home school my children and spend my happy energy being with them. Then again, that's the life I'd always wanted with Chuck and felt robbed of.

Now, there's nothing that says I can't have that, but I know in my heart it's time for me to take the responsibility and put my strengths in action by moving forward with my life. It's time for me to set good examples of strength for my children, especially for Charlie Anne. I want them both to see that if they are ever faced with any challenges, big or small, they can heal from it and not get stuck in the muck of fearful emotions. I always like what our co-author Trish says, and I need to remember this more often: "You can't drive forward while looking in the rearview mirror!" It is so true, and I'm ready to put the car in drive and move forward.

Taking action to do the things I really want to do is another way I'll be creating opportunities for next year. I see myself applying my newfound strengths by participating or even hosting Ayurvedic weekend workshops or seminars along with my own Ayurvedic business during the week. I can set my own fee schedule and work while the kids are in school. I see my workplace surrounded by loving and kind people that are also serving others. Perhaps it will be a co-op type of healing business.

Where I'm at right now, that looks like a lot to accomplish in a year, but then again, is it really? I'm going to put this to the test. I'm going to do my best to remain open and receptive to my inner divine guidance as well as grounded enough to be able to take action and trust the process. That's living life in balance. It truly is the life I want and the life I am going to strive for. Ultimately, it's my choice, and this is what I'm choosing.

EPILOGUE

Trish is working on several books and a documentary project about the connection between mind, body, and spirit. She is available for speaking and workshops at trish@wonderwidows.com. Trish continues to devote time to the nonprofit she and Bob founded, North Campus Community Project (www.nccpnm.org), which focuses on building a thriving and sustainable community for all ages. She enjoys time with her children, grandchildren, and friends.

Peggy also savors time with her children, grandchildren, and friends. She maintains a strong involvement with her essential oil business (www.peggyoils.com) and her business associates. She consciously strives to keep stress to a minimum while serving others, taking care of herself, and traveling. The trip to Africa was a good-for-the-soul trip. Being in the presence of wild animals roaming free had a very calming effect on Estelle and Peggy. She is researching creative and environmentally pleasing methods of dealing with Dan's cremation remains, or cremains.

Jennifer is now exploring new ways to recreate community that will help support living a fuller and more productive life, including raising healthy children and honoring Elders.

Estelle, invited to the Wonder Widows roundtable by Peggy, started out as one of the original four Wonder Widows. Eventually, Estelle made the decision to focus on her grown children, her grandchildren, and her aging mother. She therefore stepped back from continuing to contribute to the book. We remain in close contact and will always have a place at the table for her.

Epilogues are often meant to be a conclusion or a summary, but as we know, all endings create new beginnings. We'd like to take this opportunity to share with our readers a continuation of our mission to break the silence of widowhood.

We have invited our sisters in widowhood to open a dialogue and share their journeys around our table, and we are extending the invitation to our supportive friends, extended family, and neighbors so they can join the conversation.

It is our intent to create a more inclusive and supportive community that will give our friends, family, and neighbors a variety of ways to express more love and compassion to those of us in our time of greatest need.

We found cards of condolences in the mail, beautiful flower arrangements at our door, and casseroles placed on our table in the days that followed. We were very grateful for the thoughtfulness. We also understood folks were going to go back to their busy lives, but we were just beginning to put one foot in front of the other. We discovered a set of new needs that often necessitated a second pair of hands, a change of scenery, or more human contact, just to name a few.

We are in the process of putting together a list of "helpful needs" for widows in the early stages of grief so that her journey from grief to joy becomes one that is supported with love and compassion while she creates her new beginning.

As always, we welcome your thoughts on what would have been most helpful for you when you were in the early stages of widowhood. Visit our website, www.wonderwidows. com, to learn how you can become involved in the project and contribute to the growing list of helpful needs.

ABOUT THE AUTHORS

Trish Comer recognized Robert as her soul mate the moment she met him while he was fulfilling an internship requirement for his degree in behavioral science at a youth service bureau in a suburb of Chicago while she was facilitating a volunteer training at the same facility. They discovered they had much in common. They shared a love of nature and practiced meditation. They both also studied the philosophy of Taoism.

The two fell in love and became engaged in just a little over a month. Five months later, they got married in a park-like, wooded area in a suburb of Chicago in May of 1978. In April of 1979, Räna was born. Their love of adventure took the young family to the mountains of western North Carolina, where their son Justin was born twenty-one months after their daughter. Trish and her family then returned to the Chicago area for seven years. There, Trish taught meditation and gave presentations and workshops on stress reduction techniques. A few short years later, she studied hypnosis and opened a practice.

Their love of adventure tugged at their heartstrings once again, and a move to Albuquerque, New Mexico was in order in 1989. While Robert settled into his position as the director of a behavioral health program at the Pueblo of Laguna, Trish opened her hypnosis practice and continued running stress reduction workshops. While preparing for a workshop, she was given a gift from her higher conscious, the visual model of harmony and balance that became the cornerstone for her subsequent workshops and the theme for her forthcoming book on the subject.

Trish and Robert trained together at the Pueblo of Laguna, eventually co-leading workshops focusing on the indigenous model called Gathering of Native Americans (GONA). The GONA model facilitates mental/emotional healing by teaching the participant how to incorporate the foundation of the model, the 4-Stages of Life, to bring harmony and balance into one's everyday life.

As an accomplished practitioner of hypnosis, the study of the mind, combined with her quest to better understand the human condition, including her own, Trish began to meditate to remain open and receptive to finding a unified method of healing that combined the mind, body, and spirit—a method that she could weave into her lifelong studies of Taoism, meditation and stress reduction, her continually evolving understanding of harmony and balance, and the 4-Stages of Life. Thus, she was led to the ancient healing art and science of Reiki. She opened the Kurama Institute of Natural Healing to teach Reiki to health care professionals to help them combine Western allopathic medicine with Eastern natural healing.

As Trish and Robert began to explore options for their second half of life, a new livelihood that mirrored the 4th Stage of Life—"Generosity" or giving back to the community began to take shape for them. They settled on combining their lifelong experiences and founded the North Campus Community Project, a grassroots, multigenerational, and all neighbor-volunteer nonprofit organization designed to build a more sustainable and thriving community for the twenty-first century.

Then, after thirty-six years of marriage Robert passed away in August of 2014. In between her grieving periods, Trish felt pulled to create a new identity for herself, while still building upon the work she and Robert had started together.

Currently, Trish is involved with the City of Albuquerque's Age-Friendly movement, a movement originally founded by the World Health Organization designed to help cities create a positive and healthy environment for all ages in the twenty-first century. Trish helped Albuquerque receive the highly coveted designation of Age-Friendly status.

Trish was recently featured in a documentary on the theme of mind, body, and spirit.

In addition to preparing for the release of the harmony and balance book, she is currently working on a manuscript consisting of a collection of short stories based on conversations between a grandfather and his grandson set in the future, during the new Age of Alignment. Also, she has designed a workshop on healing grief to help rediscover the joy in life once again.

Trish is available for speaking and workshops at
trish@wonderwidows.com

Peggy Langenwalter married her prince charming in 1970 when she was eighteen years old. She was spending the summer of 1969 in the Bedford, Massachusetts area where her father had been transferred by the Raytheon Company in January 1969. When her father moved east, Peggy, her mother, and younger brother and sister stayed in southern New Mexico until the school year ended in May. After a month or two of exploring the beautiful eastern states and visiting relatives in New York, Peggy took a summer job at Raytheon, where she met a handsome young man who had also taken a job there after completing his tour with the Navy.

Peggy became a widow when Dan died unexpectedly while Peggy was out of town on business. They had happily celebrated their forty-second anniversary the week before.

While married, Peggy spent many years as a stay-at-home mom, taking care of hearth, home, and children. Her interest in complementary healing modalities began around age five and was woven into her busy life as wife and mother. Eventually, as the nest thinned and emptied, Peggy's interest in learning and sharing natural healing methods received more focus, grew into a massage practice, and then blossomed into a thriving business which highlights the use of superior quality essential oils for therapeutic purposes. She feels she has the best job in the world because she gets rewarded for being nice to people and helping them enjoy life more fully.

Peggy and Dan lived in Chelmsford, Massachusetts; Albuquerque, New Mexico; Tehran, Iran. They went back to Albuquerque, then to Evergreen, Colorado, and finally decided to return to Albuquerque to finish raising their three sons and eventually retire from working. Life took its sudden turn and the retirement plan did not happen, but Albuquerque provides a friendly and good environment for Peggy to create her new chapter of life.

For further information, Peggy can be contacted at peggy@wonderwidows.com

Jennifer Cox-Horak met her soul mate and eloped on April Fools Day of 2004. Jennifer was thirty-one and hailed from Orange, Texas, and Chuck was forty-six, residing in Fort Stockton, Texas, near Austin. Their journey took the two to Albuquerque because Jennifer wanted to study under Doctor Lad at the Ayurvedic Institute. Dr. Lad's books kept appearing in her path and guiding her to Albuquerque. Jennifer was passionate about understanding the connection between the mind, body, and spirit.

Jennifer is a certified lifestyle consultant. She is also certified in Ayuryoga, which enables her to customize lifestyle changes per individual need.

After Chuck's death in 2010, Jennifer studied postpartum Ayurvedic Doula work along with massage therapy and received certification as a Core Synchronization therapist. The latter half of her studies occurred because of her experience with Chuck's death and her need to provide information and paths for others that have experienced various forms of challenge in their life.

Jennifer can be contacted at jennifer@wonderwidows.com

APPENDIX I

…And Your Story?

We have been blessed by so much healing while we wrote our stories that we thought it could be just as beneficial for you to tell your story too, even if you keep the story to yourself.

Take a little time and think about each of the questions. Some may not apply to your situation, but answer the ones that do. If you wish to share your answers with us, we invite you to do so. You can email the Wonder Widows at info@wonderwidows.com or visit our website at www.wonderwidows.com and join in the conversation at our blog, Wonder Words.

1. <u>Did You Feel It Coming?</u>
Did you have any interesting intuitions, premonitions or conversations before death or illness?

2. <u>Cremation or Burial?</u>
What did you decide to do with the body?

3. <u>Memorial or Celebration of Life?</u>
Was it somber or celebratory?

4. Support System
Did friends and family come to your aid?
Is there anyone special that stood by your side?

5. Am I Losing My Mind?
Describe your variation of brain fog caused by grief.
Did you use alcohol or other substances to cope? If not, what did you do to best cope with your grief?

6. I Miss You!
Describe the activities that you and your husband would have enjoyed.
Do you miss eating or preparing food with your husband?
Were you drawn to certain literature?
Did you visit places your husband enjoyed or was connected to?
What would you do if you had one more day with your husband?

7. Messages From Him
Did you have dreams or animal messengers? If so, what were they and describe their significance.

8. Help! I Can't Do This Alone
Did you, or do you, feel vulnerable being alone?
Who has come to your aid?

9. Philosophy
What are your strengths, wisdom and beliefs that helped you then and are helping you now?

10. Creating My Own Space
What conscious decisions did you make to move from "our space" to "my space"?

11. Sex and the Reluctant Single Woman
Do you consider yourself a single woman?
Are you ready for dating?
Do you still wear your wedding ring?
Have you tried a dating website? If so, describe your experience.
Have you been "hit on" by others? If so, what did it feel like?

12. Self-Care
Have you given yourself permission to rest? If so, describe how you are resting and healing.

13. Creating a New Identity
What steps have you taken to create a new identity?

14. And Here Come the Holidays and Anniversaries
Describe all the first milestones and how they felt. How did you feel in year two and beyond?

15. Odd Coincidences
Have you experienced any quirky connections between life and death?

16. Looking at the Bright Side of Being a Widow
Describe any positive feelings and/or experiences that widowhood has brought to you.
Describe the positive things that life has brought to you since your spouse has passed.

17. Your Children and Grandchildren
If you have children and or grandchildren, what were their thoughts about the passing?
How did they view you within the first year of the passing of your spouse?

18. Where Do You See Yourself In One Year?
This is a fun visual exercise where you can utilize the power of your imagination. You will want to find a quiet moment to investigate all possible futures that you can create from your imagination. What would you like your future to look like? Does the image of your future feel really good? Does it make you feel powerful? Do you feel more at peace? Do you feel love and joy in your heart once again? Once you have narrowed the future you want to create down to one "story" that resonates or excites you enough from within, describe in detail what you want your next year or beyond to look like. Be flexible if your thoughts of your future take a different turn or change. Remember, life is truly a journey!

APPENDIX II

Books We Found Helpful:

I Wasn't Ready To Say Goodbye: Surviving, Coping, & Healing After the Sudden Death of a Loved One, by Brook Noel and Pamela D. Blair, PhD, Sourcebooks, Inc., Naperville, IL, updated edition, originally published in 2000 by Champion Press.

The Second Half of Life: Opening the Eight Gates of Wisdom, by Angeles Arrien, Sounds True, Boulder, CO, 2005.

Saturday Night Widows: The Adventures of Six Friends Remaking Their Lives, by Becky Aikman, Crown Publishers, New York, 2013.

The Happiness Project, by Gretchen Rubin, originally published December 2009.

Nobody Likes a Cockblock, by R. Swanson, an adult book written in children's style about woodland creature moms and dads just trying to get their groove on, Osun Books, 2016.

The Top Ten Things Dead People Want to Tell YOU, by Mike Dooley, Hay House, Oct 2014.

We realize men lose spouses and partners, too. For widowers and those who care about them, we recommend a wonderful book authored by Peggy's cousin, Herb Knoll: The Widower's Journey, Helping Men Rebuild After Their Loss. CreateSpace Independent Publishing Platform, 2017, by Herb Knoll with Deborah Carr, PhD and Robert L. Frick.

APPENDIX III

Helpful Tips
Guidelines For Healing Grief

1. **Talk about it.** Share your grief within the family—do not attempt to protect family members by silence. Find a friend to talk to, someone who will listen without passing judgment. If possible, find someone who has experienced a similar sorrow. Talk often. If the friend tells you to "snap out of it," find another friend.

2. **Keep busy.** Do purposeful work that occupies the mind but avoid frantic activity.

3. **Take care of yourself.** Bereavement can be a threat to your health. At the moment you may feel you don't care. That will change. You are important. Your life is valuable; care for it.**Eat well.** At this time of emotional and physical depletion, your body needs good nourishment more than ever. If you can only manage to pick at your food, a vitamin supplement regimen might be helpful but it will not make up for a poor diet. Be good to yourself.

4. Exercise regularly. Return to your old program or start a new one as soon as possible. Depression can be lightened by the biochemical changes brought about by exercise. Exercise will also help you sleep better. An hour long walk everyday is ideal for many people.

5. Get rid of imagined guilt. You did the best you could at the time, all things considered. If you feel you were mistaken, learn to accept that we are all imperfect. Only hindsight is 20-20. If you are convinced that you have real guilt, consider professional or spiritual counseling. If you follow a religion, a clergy may help you accept forgiveness.

6. Accept your understanding of the death. You have probably asked "why" over and over and have finally realized you will get no acceptable answer. Most likely, you have some small degree of understanding. Use that as your viewpoint until you are able to work up to another level of understanding.

7. Find a person or group of others who are sorrowing. Your old circle of friends may change. Even if it does not, you will need new friends who have been through your experience. Bereaved people sometimes form groups for friendship and sharing.

APPENDIX IV

Helpful Tips
Appropriate Expectations You Can Have For
Yourself In Grief

Your grief will take longer than most people think.

Your grief will take more energy than you would have ever imagined.

Your grief will involve many changes and be continually developing.

Your grief will show itself in all spheres of your life: psychological, social, and physical. Response to a major loss is more global than we are prepared for.

Your grief will depend on how you perceive the loss.

You will grieve for many things both symbolic and tangible, not just the death alone.

You will grieve for what you have already lost and for what you have lost for the future.

Your grief will entail mourning not only for the actual person you lost but also for all the hopes, dreams, and unfulfilled expectations you held for and with that person, and for the needs that will go unmet because of the death.

Your grief will involve a wide variety of feelings and reactions, not solely those that are generally thought of as grief, such as depression and sadness.

The loss will resurrect old issues, feelings and unresolved conflicts from the past.

You will have some identity confusion as a result of this major loss and will probably experience reactions that may be quite different for you.

You may feel a combination of anger and depression, such as irritability, frustration, annoyance, or intolerance.

You may have a lack of self-concern.

You may experience grief spasms, acute upsurges of grief that occur suddenly, with no warning.

You will have trouble thinking and making decisions. Memory, organization, and intellectual processing are affected.

You may feel like you are going crazy.

You may be obsessed with the death and preoccupied with the deceased.

You may begin a search for meaning and may question your religion, faith, or philosophy of life.

You may find yourself acting socially in ways different from before.

You may find yourself having a number of physical reactions.

Society will have unreal expectations about your mourning and may respond inappropriately to you.

You may find there are certain dates, events, and stimuli such as a special song, location, phrase, or scent that brings upsurges of grief.

Certain experiences or events later in life may resurrect intense grief for you temporarily.